Stepping Inside

BUILDING SPIRITUAL MUSCLE

1/16/22

Dear Chloe,
Trust your relationship with God!
XoXo,
Serene Shaleen

ENJOY YOUR
SPIRITUAL JOURNEY

SERENE SHALEEN

WWW.SERENESHALEEN.COM

D0819359

Shaleen Makhijani-Shivdasani

Stepping Inside

BUILDING SPIRITUAL MUSCLE

A DAILY INSPIRATIONAL JOURNEY UTILIZING
EMOTIONAL GROWTH TO BECOME SPIRITUALLY STRONG

Shaleen Makhijani-Shivdasani

PAGE PUBLISHING, INC.
Conneaut Lake, PA

First originally published by Page Publishing 2021

ISBN 978-1-6624-4517-0 (pbk)
ISBN 978-1-6624-4519-4 (hc)
ISBN 978-1-6624-4518-7 (digital)

Printed in the United States of America

Dedication

To my wonderful husband, **Shyam**,

We have been on an incredible journey since 1991 of love, joy, sorrow, the births of our two beautiful sons, Shaan and Krishin, caregiving, traveling, and most of all—being there for each other with love, admiration, respect, trust and faith. Our mutual support of each other's dreams is truly a gift.

To my handsome first born, **Shaan**,

God helped you make me a mum. You have brought laughter, love and spiritual growth to me. You are the pride of my life (Shaan means "pride" in Hindi) and our family. Your journey in your young life has shown me just how much gratitude one can achieve through the challenges one faces. You have led by example about giving back and paying it forward. Your most inspiring character trait is your deep empathy for others.

To my beautiful baby of our family, **Krishin**,

You are the quiet one, who taught me how to take things slow (KST—Krishin Standard Time). You also taught me it is okay to say, "I Don't Know." You said it so often, way before "IDK" was part of texting lingo. You have come out of your quiet shell to become an amazingly kind and dedicated soul. Your strength is your willingness to learn.

My three men and myself are a family of GIVERS. I have accepted and admired the awareness and ability of my family to give to themselves FIRST and then to others. In addition, this family's acceptance of a Higher Power, namely God, to provide and nurture the spiritual foundation in each of us, is shared outwardly for others to see how God can work in their own lives.

Foreword

This book is a gift 🎁 that I give to each of you. The purpose of this daily reader/journal is to help you discover who you are, what your purpose in life is, and to deepen your spiritual connection with God. God loves you and wants to spend time watching you get to know yourself.

This daily reader can be used as a gratitude journal as well. On every page, there is space for the reader to set their intentions for the day and to write their gifts of gratitude from the day. The reader will discover how many intentions can be set and uncover all the many blessings they have in their life.

Many of these thoughts were written during times of struggle when my spiritual connection needed to become a stronghold for me. Some of these thoughts came when I was on vacation, at church or temple, resting in bed, in the middle of my workday, or simply enjoying life. Others were written when a loved one's life was in the balance. These inspirational writings allowed me to shift from struggle to serenity.

How this book can be used is a very personal preference. Some may use it as a daily reader, others may use it as a gratitude journal. Some may use it as both. For me the purpose is simple: to share the spiritual messages and gifts of positivity, love, faith, hope and gratitude with all who read them.

My prayer for the reader is simple. I pray that as a result of using this daily journal/reader, the individual deepens their own spiritual connection with God through their emotional growth.

Now let the incredible journey of spiritual growth and emotional stamina begin and enjoy the presence of God along the way.

Take the time, to re-read the thoughts 🗩, your intentions and gifts 🎁 of gratitude and watch your spirit continue to blossom, like a beautiful lotus flower ✿—blooming in the murkiest of water. ❋

My only request to you, the reader, is to share a copy of the book with anyone who could benefit from taking the **STEPS** into their own spiritual journey.

Shaleen Makhijani-Shivdasani
Aka
Serene Shaleen

JANUARY

BREATHE

January 1ˢᵗ

Morning - Serenity

Serenity and spiritual growth are directly correlated. As I grow spiritually, my serenity grows. My ability to maintain my serenity increases.

My Intent For Today:

1.

2.

3.

Evening - The New Me

Each new year is an opportunity to grow into the person I want to be with each new day. When I see what I want to improve in myself and what I want to change, I am taking the first step towards becoming a better version of me. It takes time and patience to become this new improved me. I know the only one who can do this for me is me and I am worth it.

Today I Am Grateful For:

1.

2.

3.

January 2nd

<u>Morning - Smile ☺</u>
SMILE means to me:
So
Many
Important
Life
Events

When I smile ☺, I guarantee someone will smile back at me. Smiling makes me feel better. I will share the warmth of my smile with the world or with just one person and make their day brighter. The gift of my smile ☺ is priceless.

My Intent For Today:
1.

2.

3.

<u>Evening - Resolutions</u>
As a new day of the New Year ends, I have hope, faith and trust in ME that I can choose to be happy! Tonight I choose happiness and I will try to share this with others.

Today I Am Grateful For:
1.

2.

3.

January 3ʳᵈ

Morning - Life's Goodness

The goodness of life is a result of the things I need to be doing and leaving everything else alone. It works.

My Intent For Today:

1.

_____

2.

_____

3.

_____

Evening - Dog and God

What we learn about life by living with a dog :

1) Live in the moment
2) Drink lots of water
3) Overcome fear with love (dogs walk away from unsafe places to go where they feel loved)
4) Play everyday
5) Detachment and growth—a litter of pups gets separated at 8 weeks
6) Jump for joy when you are happy
7) Do not hold grudges (dogs will fight one moment and be playing in the next moment)
8) Enjoy the journey (dogs love car rides, heads out the window, smelling the air and feeling the wind against their faces)
9) Accept yourself (a shih tzu does not try to be like a golden doodle, etc.)
10) Life goes on after they leave us … they teach us about LOSS
11) Be loyal and dependable
12) Love unconditionally

Today I Am Grateful For:

1.

_____

2.

_____

3.

_____

January 4ᵗʰ

Morning - Life is a Gift 🎁

Today is another beautiful day to enjoy life as it unfolds. God has plans for me and I trust God knows exactly what I need. The gift 🎁 I give myself today is to love God as God loves me UNCONDITIONALLY and ALWAYS.

My Intent For Today:

1.

_____

2.

_____

3.

_____

Evening - Forgiveness

Forgiveness does not create a relationship. Unless people speak the truth about what they have done and change their minds and behaviors, a relationship of trust is not possible. When I forgive someone I certainly release them from judgment, but without the change, no real relationship can be established. I can forgive and still never forget, nor do I have to. I can learn to love them in the face of it and begin to build a bridge of reconciliation.

Today I Am Grateful For:

1.

_____

2.

_____

3.

_____

January 5th

Morning - Control
The only kinds of control I want are Cruise Control and Climate Control. Both serve me well on those long drives, whether a cold winter or a hot summer day.

My Intent For Today:
1.

_____

2.

_____

3.

_____

Evening - Tears
Tears can be healing waters and a stream of joy. Sometimes tears are the best words the heart can speak. Tears are cleansing and a healthy way to relieve unhealthy emotions and stress. Tears are a sign of courage, strength and authenticity. Tears are a way to relax emotions. Let the tears flow to de-stress and remove negativity.

Today I Am Grateful For:
1.

_____

2.

_____

3.

_____

January 6th

Morning - Hope, Fear and God

God is always here to serve me. I am the one who refuses to be served. This right of refusal never serves me well. My relationship with God was established at my birth and never ends even when I think God has forgotten me. Usually when I feel God has forgotten me, it is me who has forgotten God. When I feel God is far away, I realize it is probably me who has moved and I can always return **HOME** to God. Fear holds me back and makes me weak. Hope moves me forward and keeps me strong.

My Intent For Today:

1.

_____

2.

_____

3.

_____

Evening - Fear and Hope

FEAR closes the doors and keeps me locked inside myself.
HOPE keeps the windows open to beautiful possibilities.

Today I Am Grateful For:

1.

_____

2.

_____

3.

_____

January 7th

Morning - Living
If I live out each day as if I were traveling on a vacation, the possibilities and discoveries are infinite. Vacations most always hold wonderful memories.

My Intent For Today:
1.

_____

2.

_____

3.

_____

Evening - Positivity
If I fill my mind with positive thoughts throughout my day there is no room for negativity. Positive thoughts lead to positive actions. It is metaphysically impossible for the human mind to process a positive thought and a negative thought at the same time. Therefore when a negative thought takes up space in my beautiful mind, I realize the rent is very high. The rent is free for positive thoughts.

Today I Am Grateful For:
1.

_____

2.

_____

3.

_____

January 8th

Morning - Feeling My Emotions

When I feel an emotion that may not be in my best interest or serve me well, I remind myself that I need to feel everything. If I block myself from feeling negative emotions, I actually do a disservice to myself. When I feel physically ill, I am aware of it and I let someone know (e.g., a loved one or a doctor). Similarly, if I am not feeling emotionally well, I need to take a pause and understand why and then perhaps I can help myself either move through it or ask for help (sometimes God's help works best). All feelings are alright; they are part of who I am and what I experience. Today I will ask for God's help when I am in need, since I know God is always there for me and loves me.

My Intent For Today:

1.

2.

3.

Evening - Trust

By trusting in God, nothing is inevitable or impossible. Trusting in God means accepting that God's plan is the best plan, which may not be my plan. It means things may happen or not happen and in God's time, not mine.

Today I Am Grateful For:

1.

2.

3.

January 9th

Morning - The Gifts I Am Born With

I am born with certain gifts. I also develop gifts as I grow. My gifts when shared with others have the benefit of perhaps lifting someone up and also help fill a void in my life. My gifts add richness to others and can be shared by others who in turn will pass the gifts to even more people. My abilities, whether it is knitting, baking, electrical work, soothing someone's hurt, being a good listener, being artistic; whatever my gift, it can be special to someone in need. Sharing my gifts allows my potential to be shared with those willing to receive the gift. Today, I will do my best to share one of my gifts with someone who is in need.

My Intent For Today:

1.

_____

2.

_____

3.

_____

Evening - Try

I only fail when I do not try!

Today I Am Grateful For:

1.

_____

2.

_____

3.

_____

January 10th

Morning - Strength and Peace

God creates beauty for ashes, strength for fear, gladness for mourning, and peace for despair.

My Intent For Today:

1.

_____

2.

_____

3.

_____

Evening - Love

LOVE means:

Letting	**L**isten	**L**iving
Others	**O**penly	**O**n
Voluntarily	**V**alue	**V**ibrant
Evolve	**E**ncourage	**E**nergy

Today I Am Grateful For:

1.

_____

2.

_____

3.

_____

January 11ᵗʰ

Morning - God's Plan

Today is another beautiful day to enjoy life as it unfolds. God has plans for me today and I trust God knows what I need for today.

My Intent For Today:

1.

_____

2.

_____

3.

_____

Evening - Forgiveness

For help with forgiveness, I can use the word REACH.
REACH means:
Recall the event
Empathize with the players
Altruism (What does God want me to do?)
Commit to the change
Heartfelt

Forgiveness takes HARD WORK and is well worth it. Self-forgiveness brings peace.

Today I Am Grateful For:

1.

_____

2.

_____

3.

_____

January 12th

Morning - Believe

When I believe, I acquire faith, trust and serenity.
BELIEVE means:
Being
Empathizing
Loving
Inspiring
Engaging
Validating
Enjoying

My life is beautiful when I BELIEVE in myself and in God!

My Intent For Today:

1.

2.

3.

Evening - Positivity

The best way for me to be positive in my actions is to think positively.
I begin my evening by reading something positive which leads to a
positive act. It is also a beautiful way to conclude my evening.

Today I Am Grateful For:

1.

2.

3.

January 13th

<u>Morning - Me Time</u>
24 hours multiplied by 60 minutes = 1,440 minutes
1% of 1,440 minutes is approximately 15 minutes

I can certainly spend 15 minutes each day for "ME" time AND for "GOD" time. At first it may be difficult, but once I make it a healthy habit, the rewards are amazing. I can even break up the 15 minutes during the day and not have to limit myself.

My Intent For Today:
1.

_____
2.

_____
3.

_____

<u>Evening - Serenity</u>
The ideal way to ensure that my serenity grows is to nurture it, feed it, and share it with others.

Today I Am Grateful For:
1.

_____
2.

_____
3.

_____

January 14ᵗʰ

Morning - Control versus Serenity

When I let go of things that are not in my control, I increase my serenity. I let these things go into the hands of God who is always in control. God can bring me more peace and serenity by taking these things off my worry list and releasing my grip.

My Intent For Today:

1.

_____

2.

_____

3.

_____

Evening - Paws and Process

Just because a problem or difficult situation may arise today, does not mean the solution must be found today. I remind myself to "PAWS ", PROCESS, and PAMPER myself.

PAWS means ~ **P**rayer, **A**cceptance, **W**isdom, **S**erenity

Today I Am Grateful For:

1.

_____

2.

_____

3.

_____

January 15th

Morning - Heal

The word **HEAL** can mean:

Healthy	Helping
Eating	Everyone
Active	Accept
Living	Love

My Intent For Today:

1.

_____

2.

_____

3.

_____

Evening - Health and Faith

I do my best to keep my body, mind and spirit focused on God's plan for me. Knowing that by keeping my faith strong, my fears weak, my heart pure, my thoughts positive, and my mind at ease, no harm can come to me. Only good things can happen. God's plan for me is the best I can ever imagine and the good news is the plan will happen whether I want it to or not. God is in control, not me. My choice is merely to be present, to be a team player on God's winning team. I know that all the choices God makes for me are in my best interest and God always knows BEST!

Today I Am Grateful For:

1.

_____

2.

_____

3.

_____

January 16th

Morning - The Seed of Faith

God gives each of us a seed of faith. This seed grows quicker in some of us than others. It takes many twists and turns to develop into the beautiful flower of ever-growing faith. In a few of us, the seed may not grow but God never loses faith in His/Her children.

My Intent For Today:

1.

_____

2.

_____

3.

_____

Evening - God is My Source

God is the source of the air I breathe, the food that nourishes my body, and the spirit that comforts my soul. I breathe in this truth. I exhale, releasing any thoughts or feelings that do not serve me well or do not keep me healthy. I feel a return to that deep inner peace that permeates my being.

With God as my constant source, I am infused with peace, strength, joy, love and gratitude. I am infused with amazing friends like YOU! I focus on being happy and sharing my happiness with those I may meet tomorrow … whether through my smile or by saying "Have a blessed day," or simply by being a better me.

Today I Am Grateful For:

1.

_____

2.

_____

3.

_____

January 17th

Morning - All About Me

God helps me look my best by supporting me on the outside and inside. Travel with me today as WE share kindness to those WE meet on today's journey. Together WE have the energy to make this happen.

My Intent For Today:

1.
_____

2.
_____

3.
_____

Evening - God is Within Me

God is within people ... not outside. This is similar to the concept of Buddha being inside each of us. The spirit of humanity is part of all of us and allows us to share and to care.

Today I Am Grateful For:

1.
_____

2.
_____

3.
_____

January 18ᵗʰ

Morning - Life

LIFE means:

Living	Love	Love
In	Is	Inspire
Faith	For	Forgive
Everyday	Everyone	Everyday

My Intent For Today:
1.

_____

2.

_____

3.

_____

Evening - Breathe

The air I breathe is not visible to me, yet it is always available for me and is essential to my life. This is the same with God. God is not visible to me; yet is always there for me and is essential to my life. I will remember this with each breath that I take. I am breathing in God's love and strength for me.

Today I Am Grateful For:
1.

_____

2.

_____

3.

_____

January 19ᵗʰ

Morning - My Feelings, My Health
Today I will honor my feelings and try my best to express myself in a way that is healthiest for me.

My Intent For Today:
1.

_____

2.

_____

3.

_____

Evening - Relationship
A relationship is like a diamond. Diamonds have four C's to determine their beauty and value: Cut, Clarity, Carat and Color. Every relationship has the **ABC**'s needed for its success:

Acceptance	Attitudes	Actions
Belief	Behaviors	Bring
Compassion	Communication	Change

Today I Am Grateful For:
1.

_____

2.

_____

3.

_____

January 20th

Morning - Pause and Process

When a situation happens or a problem is brought to my attention, especially one that does not directly involve me, I realize it is important for me to pause and process. There is absolutely no need for me to act/react right away. It is most beneficial for me to take my time to digest the information that I have just become aware of, accept the situation, and then take action. This way I am not acting out of emotion and my actions have thought behind them. If I realize that the situation/problem probably took time to happen, thus my action/reaction too, can take time to happen. Today I will take my time in processing situations and act/react accordingly. I will do my best to underreact. I will work at improving/strengthening my emotional stamina.

My Intent For Today:

1.

_____

2.

_____

3.

_____

Evening - Peace

Peace is a gift that I give myself by keeping drama out of my life ... if drama enters the room, I can choose to walk away. Drama is much better watched in a movie, TV show or mini-series. I have the POWER to turn it off or keep watching.

Today I Am Grateful For:

1.

_____

2.

_____

3.

_____

January 21ˢᵗ

Morning - My Life

My life continues to evolve as I discover new things about myself. With God's help I will find out which things are worth exploring more and developing further.

My Intent For Today:

1.

_____

2.

_____

3.

_____

Evening - Saying No

I will do my best to be willing to say NO when I need to; especially, when to do so will maintain my inner peace and serenity.

Today I Am Grateful For:

1.

_____

2.

_____

3.

_____

January 22nd

Morning - Being Still

Even in the midst of a busy office or a noisy marketplace, I can be still and know that I am one with God. I let the chatter in my mind surrender to stillness and silence. Today I stay in contact with God and know that I am loved, protected, and cared for at all times.

My Intent For Today:

1.

_____

2.

_____

3.

_____

Evening - Three Parts to My Health

All my emotions help me to grow. The positive emotions allow me to feel calm, refreshed and grateful. The negative emotions also serve a purpose. They help me to work at improving how I express them. This takes both work and practice and is very rewarding. Emotions need to be expressed in a way that keeps me physically and spiritually healthy. My health has three parts: emotional, physical and spiritual. Each part interacts with the other two and no one part is more important. Like an equilateral triangle, each component of my health has an equal part. All three make up the whole.

Today I Am Grateful For:

1.

_____

2.

_____

3.

_____

January 23ʳᵈ

Morning - I Am Great
I am feeling **GREAT** means:
God
Respectfully
Encourages
Absolute
Trust

My Intent For Today:
1.
_____
2.
_____
3.
_____

Evening - Gratitude Assessment
The nightly assessment of gratitude from the day's activity leads to mental and spiritual growth. It also reduces stress and negative thinking. A gratitude assessment cultivates healthier relationships. It provides goodness and positivity in one's life. Most of all the expression of gratitude improves one's overall health and well-being. Gratitude does not cost a thing, but pays handsomely in its rewards and benefits.

Today I Am Grateful For:
1.
_____
2.
_____
3.
_____

January 24th

Morning - Listen

Listen with the ears of your heart and soul.
See with the eyes of your soul.
Speak with the voice of the Spirit within you.

My Intent For Today:

1.

_____

2.

_____

3.

_____

Evening - Trust in God

My dreams can come true if I have the courage to pursue them. I trust in God and work hard.

Today I Am Grateful For:

1.

_____

2.

_____

3.

_____

January 25th

Morning - Keeping Healthy

Today I choose to use God to help me make healthy choices, to use tools that will keep me healthy. It is in keeping myself healthy that I can be of good use to others who may ask or need my help. I will share this choice with others.

My Intent For Today:

1.

_____

2.

_____

3.

_____

Evening - Relationships

Relationships are simple if I keep them simple. One way to improve a relationship is to define my role and what I may need to change. If I make even the slightest change, the other person will either respond to the change or continue as they are. If I stick to my change and be consistent, this will work. If not, then I will know I have tried my best. All my relationships have a purpose. I learn from all my relationships. I can learn more about myself from my relationships. The relationship I can count on always is the one I have with God. This one always works and will always last.

Today I Am Grateful For:

1.

_____

2.

_____

3.

_____

January 26th

Morning - God Always

God always loves us

God always has the best plans for us

God always is with us

God always promises us life, whether here on Earth or eternal life in Heaven

God always forgives us

God always thinks about us

God never gets tired

God never takes on a task He/She cannot handle

God never tires of taking care of us

God never judges us

God can do all of these things all the time and it takes the pressure off us trying to be God

My Intent For Today:

1.

_____

2.

_____

3.

_____

Evening - Happiness

Tonight I focus on being happy and preparing to share my happiness with those I will meet tomorrow. I will do this through my smile or by simply saying "Have a blessed day" or being a better me.

Today I Am Grateful For:

1.

_____

2.

_____

3.

_____

January 27th

Morning - Flexibility

Today I will be more flexible with my mind and experience life as it unfolds. I realize this allows me to navigate through life more freely. My flexible mind becomes less rigid and more open to change.

My Intent For Today:

1.

_____

2.

_____

3.

_____

Evening - Mindfulness and Meditation

The mind is a wonderful tool for thinking, but it has a dark side. There is an aspect of the mind that is not useful, which is called the EGOIC mind. Sometimes our mind takes us to places of judgment of others, to places of self-doubt, or even to places where our thoughts are actually those of others and not our own. Meditation helps us to quiet our minds and LISTEN to God. It allows God's guidance to help us understand our thoughts better and take appropriate actions that align with God's will for us.

Today I Am Grateful For:

1.

_____

2.

_____

3.

_____

January 28ᵗʰ

<u>Morning - Letting Go</u>
Letting go is hard to do. I realize that sometimes the best thing for me to do is: Nothing. Doing nothing is doing something.

My Intent For Today:
1.

2.

3.

<u>Evening - God as Parent</u>
The same way it is difficult for a parent to allow their crying baby to soothe themselves to sleep, so is it for God as Parent to comfort us when we are in pain.

Today I Am Grateful For:
1.

2.

3.

January 29ᵗʰ

Morning - Zero

ZERO is a number with no beginning and no end. It represents the circle of life. It can also represent God's unconditional love for me. There is great comfort in knowing that God's love for me is infinite.

My Intent For Today:

1.

_____

2.

_____

3.

_____

Evening - Love ♡ and Hugs 🤗

The best way to tell someone I love ♡ them without saying a word is to **HUG** them! I will give someone I love or care about a **HUG** today. **HUGS** 🤗 let people know they matter.

HUGS mean:

Hugs	**H**ealing
Usually	**U**nderstanding
Give	**G**enerosity
Strength	**S**piritual connections

Today I Am Grateful For:

1.

_____

2.

_____

3.

_____

January 30th

Morning - God Trusts Me

God loves me, even when I do not love me. God trusts me, even when I do not trust myself. God believes in me, even when I do not believe in myself. So when I need love, trust and someone to believe in me, I turn to GOD ... it is that EASY.

My Intent For Today:
1.

_____

2.

_____

3.

_____

Evening - Letting Go

Sometimes I need to let go instead of holding on. Other times I do need to hold on and not let go. I am learning when to let go and when to hold on. I am learning to hold on to my faith and let go of my fear. I am learning to not let go of my trust in God's plans for me and also not hold on to resentment. I am holding on to God's reign on my life's journey and I am letting go of my need to control the journey. By letting go of my need to control, I also let go of fear. I am holding on to hope and letting go of anger. Letting go feels good.

Today I Am Grateful For:
1.

_____

2.

_____

3.

_____

January 31st

Morning - Letting Go of the Past

Today I will let go of the past but this does not mean I forget the pain. I simply release it and allow God to bear my pain because God can bear it better than I can. Today I become active in making this day full of positivity so that by tomorrow, today's positivity becomes my new past. Finally, once I am successful at this task, I know that I can repeat it again tomorrow. This is the part of my life that is in my control and with God's help and unconditional love—anything and all things are truly possible. God is great all the time!

My Intent For Today:

1.

_____

2.

_____

3.

_____

Evening - Goodbye

The one thing that is sadder than saying goodbye, is not having said hello. So in the words of Lionel Richie and Adele ... HELLO!

HELLO means:

Hello

Everyone

Live

Life

Openly

Today I Am Grateful For:

1.

_____

2.

_____

3.

_____

FEBRUARY

COMPASSION

February 1st

Morning - Wonderful or Not So Good Moments

Each moment of every day counts. It can count for something wonderful or for something not so good. The "wonderful" is for my gratitude and the "not so good moments" are for the lessons I learn. Either way it is a WIN-WIN! So I try to make every moment count, and not count on every moment.

My Intent For Today:

1.

_____

2.

_____

3.

_____

Evening - Giving Thanks and Grace

Tonight I will open my heart, mind, body and most of all my hands to be thankful for all the things I experience in this beautiful life. Giving thanks and having an attitude of gratitude keeps me happy in the moment. The true grace comes when I am thankful even in my life's dark times. Being thankful when I am feeling sadness is especially challenging and yet when I can do this I feel incredibly full. Grace means favor. So the next time I ask, "Can you do me a favor?" I am really asking for Grace. Today I will work harder to be full of **GRACE** and have an attitude of **GRATITUDE**. I will share my gratitude with all those who cross my path today.

Today I Am Grateful For:

1.

_____

2.

_____

3.

_____

February 2nd

Morning - Absolute Bliss

Today I will soak my mind, body and soul in the BLESSINGS of my life which lead me to absolute BLISS, peace and serenity.

My Intent For Today:

1.

2.

3.

Evening - Forgiveness

Forgiveness is for ME; to give me peace and harmony; to release the pain I am suffering. Forgiveness is a way of being kind to myself and a way to love myself.

Today I Am Grateful For:

1.

2.

3.

February 3rd

Morning - God's Purpose

God has a purpose for my pain, a reason for my struggles, and the gift of God's presence for my faithfulness. I will never give up or let go of God. Amen.

My Intent For Today:

1.

_____

2.

_____

3.

_____

Evening - Zero

ZERO means:

Zero

Expectations

Re-energizes

Oneself

Today I Am Grateful For:

1.

_____

2.

_____

3.

_____

February 4th

Morning - Acceptance and Resistance

To me, the opposite of acceptance is resistance. Acceptance brings me much closer to God. Resistance only keeps God at an unhealthy distance. There is, at times, a tug of war between resistance and acceptance. I am growing and with each day my acceptance gives me serenity. My decreased resistance gives me peace.

My Intent For Today:

1.

_____

2.

_____

3.

_____

Evening - Bringing Everything

Tonight I bring my everything: my love, joy, pain, sorrow and life. I bring all of me to GOD!

Today I Am Grateful For:

1.

_____

2.

_____

3.

_____

February 5ᵗʰ

Morning - Love, Self-Care and Choices

Today I look to those in my life who can give me the love that I need. If someone is unable to love me at that moment, it is important to seek the love I need from God or within. This is different, difficult, and also self-caring. I can choose to share the love I am in need of with others whom I feel will appreciate the love, instead of seeking love for myself. Choices, we all have choices.

My Intent For Today:

1.

_____

2.

_____

3.

_____

Evening - Faith

FAITH means:

Faith	Failure	Forgiveness	Forward
Always	Allows	Assures	All
Instills	Inspiration	Inner-peace	Issues
Tranquil	To	To	To
Health	Happen	Happen	Heaven

Today I Am Grateful For:

1.

_____

2.

_____

3.

_____

February 6ᵗʰ

Morning - Keeping Life Simple

When I keep my life simple, my thoughts become less complicated. This is not easy to do, it takes work, and the rewards are PRICELESS. So today I practice **KISS**:

Keeping
It
So
Simple

My Intent For Today:

1.
_____
2.
_____
3.
_____

Evening - Acts of Love

Tonight, I remind myself that acts of love and kindness do not require repayment. They are the fringe benefits of a solid relationship.

Today I Am Grateful For:

1.
_____
2.
_____
3.
_____

February 7ᵗʰ

Morning - God's Rain

I think of rain as God showering love upon me. Then even the heaviest rain seems OK.

My Intent For Today:

1.
_____

2.
_____

3.
_____

Evening - Patience

PATIENCE means:

Peaceful
Accepting
Trusting
Insightful
Encouraging
Negotiable/Nurturing
Compassionate
Everlasting/Enjoyment

Today I Am Grateful For:

1.
_____

2.
_____

3.
_____

February 8ᵗʰ

Morning - Kindness and Compassion

God listens when I speak. God feels when I share myself with Him/Her. God sees my blind faith. God trusts and believes in me even when I cannot. God loves me unconditionally.

God loves me without any expectation of me returning the love. God plans the best for me even when I am not at my best. God sees my potential, when I cannot. Lastly, God guides me and does all the above with kindness and compassion. Every coin and paper currency in the US says "In God We Trust" and I do trust in God.

My Intent For Today:

1.
_____

2.
_____

3.
_____

Evening - Positivity

Tonight, as I rest and plan for tomorrow, I will do my best to stay positive in my thinking and even more positive in my ACTIONS.

Today I Am Grateful For:

1.
_____

2.
_____

3.
_____

February 9ᵗʰ

Morning - The Gifts of ...

Some gifts in my life are absolutely priceless. These are the gifts of ... serenity, peace, love and compassion. These are gifts that keep on giving me immense JOY when I open up my heart, mind, body and soul to receive them. These are gifts that I can re-use all the time. **JOY** allows me to:

Just	**J**oyfully
Open	**O**wn
Yourself	**Y**our part

My Intent For Today:
1.

_____

2.

_____

3.

_____

Evening - Being Compassionate

I am the most beautiful when I am being compassionate to myself first and then to others around me.

Today I Am Grateful For:
1.

_____

2.

_____

3.

_____

February 10th

Morning - The Power of Light

When a storm causes a power outage, it causes me to search for the light vis a vis candles, flashlights, etc. I realize that the light also comes from within me. A pilot light is always inside me and I can use it to light my way out of the darkness.

My Intent For Today:

1.

_____

2.

_____

3.

_____

Evening - Blind Faith

My blind faith gives me insight to the depth of my mind, heart, body and soul. This faith leads me to a deeper understanding of myself. Blind faith also is all about BELIEVING in things my eyes simply cannot see.

Today I Am Grateful For:

1.

_____

2.

_____

3.

_____

February 11ᵗʰ

Morning - God's Children

God presented Himself/Herself to me through the birth of my children. For me, my children are always God in the flesh. This is how God comes to me—so each day I know He/She is with me—through the lives of my children. My children can come in the form of humans, canines, felines, birds, hamsters and many more species.

My Intent For Today:

1.

_____

2.

_____

3.

_____

Evening - Rainbows 🌈 of Hope

Rainbows 🌈 appear in clouds after a heavy thunderstorm. It is God's way of showing us that we all have storms on our journeys but also have rainbows of hope in our lives. These rainbows can appear in the form of the people that travel with us on our journey. Thus, in the words of Maya Angelou, "I want to be a rainbow in someone's cloud."

Today I Am Grateful For:

1.

_____

2.

_____

3.

_____

February 12ᵗʰ

Morning - Stay Positive

Today I will do my best to stay positive in my thinking and even more positive in my actions. The best way for me to stay positive is to be positive.

My Intent For Today:

1.

_____

2.

_____

3.

_____

Evening - My Attitude of Gratitude

I will focus on my attitude of gratitude and share this with all those I encounter on my journey. I will express this in my physical appearance so that others can see exactly how I feel. I will also express my emotions in a healthy, positive manner.

Today I Am Grateful For:

1.

_____

2.

_____

3.

_____

February 13th

Morning - How I Am Feeling

When I really want to examine how I am feeling, I turn my attention and focus on my breathing. The pace and length of my breaths are a good indication of how I am feeling.

My Intent For Today:

1.

_____

2.

_____

3.

_____

Evening - Meditation as a Tool

The same way a massage relaxes one's body, meditation is the way to relax one's mind. It is important to take care of one's overall health: physically, emotionally and spiritually. Meditation increases one's spiritual health, which in turn increases both physical and emotional health. Meditation is a tool we can use to slowly dim our minds, like a dimmer switch on a light.

Today I Am Grateful For:

1.

_____

2.

_____

3.

_____

February 14ᵗʰ

Morning - Valentine's 💗 Day!

Valentine's Day. Today is that special day to show that someone special just how much you love them. Today is that special day to do something extra special for that someone special in your life. Today is the day I make sure to do something special to show that someone special just how much they mean to me, how much I love them. That someone special is ME! Today, I make sure I love ME. I take care of ME. I do something special for ME. I appreciate ME. I believe in ME. I am grateful for ME. I am true to ME. I make extra time for ME!

My Intent For Today:

1.

_____

2.

_____

3.

_____

Evening - What is Love 💗?

On a day like today, a day dedicated to love, it is essential for me to remember that when I accept those whom I love as they are, without wanting to change them, I find more inner peace. When I love without condition, I am a happier, more serene person. When I learn to truly **LOVE**, I ...

Let
Others
Voluntarily
Evolve

I remember to include myself in this kind of love. Others who love me, need to let me voluntarily evolve as well.

Today I Am Grateful For:

1.

_____

2.

_____

3.

_____

February 15th

Morning - The Anger Emotion

Anger or sadness are emotions just like excitement or joy. Today I trust myself to express my emotion of anger or sadness in a healthy way. I know that by expressing it, I am not only validating what I am feeling, I am also releasing the negative emotion from within me with the hope of replenishing myself with positive energy.

My Intent For Today:

1.

_____

2.

_____

3.

_____

Evening - God Guide Me

Today I will let God truly guide me in the dance of life because dancing is fun. If God guides me, life will be fun.
Guidance can mean:
God
U and
I
DANCE together in life—everywhere.

Today I Am Grateful For:

1.

_____

2.

_____

3.

_____

February 16ᵗʰ

Morning - When I Cannot ... God Can

Sometimes when I find I do absolutely nothing about something that is on my plate, that is actually doing something. Or a way of doing something when I really feel it is best to do nothing, is to PRAY and turn over the "doing something" to God. God is much better equipped to handle things when I cannot.

My Intent For Today:

1.

2.

3.

Evening - Feed My Soul

On this day, I will do something loving for myself. I will feed my soul with positive energy. I will spend time relaxing for a short while utilizing this time to take care of my entire being physically, emotionally and spiritually. This day will not come again and I want to be able to say I did something good for myself. If I am not successful in this endeavor, I will be kind and gentle to myself knowing that by the act of trying I indeed was successful.

Today I Am Grateful For:

1.

2.

3.

February 17th

Morning - Unhealthy Directions

If I allow my mind to wander in unhealthy directions and spend too much time thinking about things that are not in my control, I waste precious time that could be spent in a healthier way for me. Today I will try my best and catch myself when this happens and be proud of myself for doing so.

My Intent For Today:

1.

_____

2.

_____

3.

_____

Evening - Lessons and Blessings

In every situation there is either a lesson or a blessing. It is up to me to learn the lesson and/or accept the blessing. My attitude of gratitude is what helps me when my life's journey begins to take an unhealthy turn. Today I will try to be mindful of the lessons and blessings I am learning through my experiences.

Today I Am Grateful For:

1.

_____

2.

_____

3.

_____

February 18th

Morning - Mistakes and Love

It has been said that change is the only constant in life. For me, in addition to change, both God's love for me and mistakes are also constants in life. I am a human being whom God created and thus God's love for me is constant. Because I am human, I am subject to making mistakes, thus mistakes will be a constant in my life. The lesson for me is: God always loves me and I will make mistakes and I am always changing. For today, I will do my best to remember this lesson. I am allowed to make mistakes. I can make changes for myself. I am continuously loved by God.

My Intent For Today:
1.

2.

3.

Evening - Moving from Fear to Faith

Fear is the opposite of faith. While fear may sometimes strike, I will not let it control me. Instead, I will activate my faith. I am strong. I am confident. I am fearless, because I have faith in the powerful love of God.

Today I Am Grateful For:
1.

2.

3.

February 19th

Morning - Measuring My Life

Today instead of using dates and times to measure my life (measuring my age, etc.), I will measure my life by the experiences I have had. I can weigh my life by both the positive moments and blessings and the negative experiences where lessons were learned. All the experiences I have help me to grow in ways only God knows are possible for me.

My Intent For Today:

1.

_____

2.

_____

3.

_____

Evening - I Grow Like a Flower

Some flowers grow best in the sun, others grow well in the shade. I will remember that God puts me where I will grow best. I thank God for every situation. God blesses me always.

Today I Am Grateful For:

1.

_____

2.

_____

3.

_____

February 20th

Morning - Calmness and Serenity

Calmness and serenity help me before, during, and after the storms that occur in my life. After every heavy rainstorm, there is often a beautiful rainbow 🌈.

My Intent For Today:

1.

2.

3.

Evening - God's Crisis Hotline

When I have a crisis of faith, it is actually a call from God's crisis **HOTLINE**, which is always available. It is up to me to accept the call and accept the faith. Sometimes when I need to call, I can simply call **1-800-DIAL-GOD**. The line may be busy. I will leave a voicemail and wait for the reply in God's time.

Today I Am Grateful For:

1.

2.

3.

February 21st

Morning - My Spiritual Charger

When I plug into my connection with God, I get spiritually recharged. In other words, God is my spiritual charger. I keep physically healthy by exercising and eating right. I keep emotionally healthy by setting time aside for me. I keep spiritually healthy by saying my "Breath Prayers." Breath prayers are simple prayers that I can say in one full breath. Some examples are:

God loves me and I love God.
I want to know You more God, teach me the way.
God created me and knows what is best for me.
You are my God and will never leave me.
God is with me and is for me right now.
God, You trust in me and love me, so I trust in You and love You, God.
God, You are the giver of life and I love You.

My Intent For Today:

1.

_____

2.

_____

3.

_____

Evening - Prayer and Meditation

Prayer is the way I honor God. I give thanks for blessings received and yet to be received. Meditation is the way I listen to God. I receive God's continued blessings and gifts.

Today I Am Grateful For:

1.

_____

2.

_____

3.

_____

February 22ⁿᵈ

Morning - My Breath is a Life Force

My breath is the very life force within me. When I breathe in, my lungs expand, my blood is oxygenated, and I am infused with energy. Breathing out, my body releases carbon dioxide that it no longer needs, cleansing me throughout. This incredible process has been repeating itself since I was born. I focus on my breath, giving thanks for the divine life force within me. I breathe deeply, filling my lungs with this healing life. As I inhale, I affirm, I am whole and well, and I hold that thought and my breath for a few seconds. I slowly and gently exhale, affirming: Thank You, God. Through this exercise, I feel cleansed and purified, ready to face the day with renewed energy, vitality and faith.

My Intent For Today:

1.

_____

2.

_____

3.

_____

Evening - Gratitude Attack

A gratitude attack is so much healthier than a heart attack. I want to bring attention to my relationships ... not TENSION.

Today I Am Grateful For:

1.

_____

2.

_____

3.

_____

February 23rd

Morning - Faith
FAITH means:

Facing	Fear	Faith
An	Always	Assures
Inner	Inhibits	Instant
Truth	True	True
Heals	Harmony	Happiness

My Intent For Today:
1.

_____

2.

_____

3.

_____

Evening - Accept Life As It Is
I am learning to accept life as it is; to let go of life as it was; and to have faith in the life that will be.

Today I Am Grateful For:
1.

_____

2.

_____

3.

_____

February 24th

Morning - Self-Care is the Best Care

Instead of saying I deserve a break, today I will actually take a break!
Putting positive thoughts into positive actions is what helps me most
to make a change for myself, to love myself, and to practice self-care.
Self-care is the best care.

My Intent For Today:

1.

_____

2.

_____

3.

_____

Evening - A Good Example

Do I want to be a good example to others, or would I rather be a
horrible warning to others of what not to be?
Tonight I choose to be a good example to me first and then to others.

Today I Am Grateful For:

1.

_____

2.

_____

3.

_____

February 25th

Morning - My Inner GPS

When I feel like I have lost God, I rely on my inner **GPS**—**G**od **P**owered **S**olutions—to guide me on the right path of faith that leads me back to God.

My Intent For Today:

1.

2.

3.

Evening - The Power of Now

The power of **NOW**, helps me stay present.
NOW means:

Nurturing   New
Over   Options
Worrying   Welcomed

Today I Am Grateful For:

1.

2.

3.

February 26th

Morning - God's Time

I do not let the fear about my future consume my life today. I will just live for now and the right things will fall into place in God's time. God's timeline is not the same as my timeline.

My Intent For Today:

1.

_____

2.

_____

3.

_____

Evening - Blessing Means:

Being present with,
Love in my heart,
Expect blessings,
Share goodness,
Shine like the sun,
Inspire someone,
Never forget that,
God is with me all the time!

Today I Am Grateful For:

1.

_____

2.

_____

3.

_____

February 27th

Morning - Love and Death

In life, there are two things that come to me uninvited … LOVE and DEATH.

I do not have control over them or when they come to me. In these situations, it is best for me to remember God's open invitation to be with Him/Her.

My Intent For Today:

1.

_____

2.

_____

3.

_____

Evening - Nothing is Something

Sometimes the best thing to do is … NOTHING.
Sometimes the best thing to say is … NOTHING.
Sometimes the best thing to listen to is … NOTHING.
Sometimes NOTHING really is … SOMETHING.

Today I Am Grateful For:

1.

_____

2.

_____

3.

_____

February 28ᵗʰ

Morning - God's Hands

When I put everything that I cannot handle alone into God's Hands, eventually I can actually see God's Hands in everything.

My Intent For Today:

1.

_____

2.

_____

3.

_____

Evening - God is Guiding Me

I will follow my heart and walk in my faith, knowing that God is walking with me always. God is guiding me, loving me, and comforting me. My eyes do not see God, my ears do not hear God, and God cannot talk to me in the way I speak with others; and yet I know God sees, hears and listens to me. This is the gift God gives to me that shows He/She cares.

Today I Am Grateful For:

1.

_____

2.

_____

3.

_____

February 29ᵗʰ

<u>Morning - Safety</u>
SAFETY means:
Serenity
Affirms
Faith
Everyday
Towards
You

My Intent For Today:
1.

2.

3.

<u>Evening - The Mirror of Life</u>
When the mirror of my life gets dirty with the fog of reality ... I just try wiping it with my faith. I begin to see a clear reflection of my dreams once again. Tonight, I will enjoy the mirror and my reflection.

Today I Am Grateful For:
1.

2.

3.

MARCH

LOVING KINDNESS

March 1st

Morning - Love is ...

Love is watching my DOG sleep and realizing how much GOD loves me. DOG is GOD spelled backwards for a reason. Both dogs and God take a pause before taking a step forward.

My Intent For Today:

1.

_____

2.

_____

3.

_____

Evening - Forgiveness Shows ...

I am learning to replace blame with forgiveness. Forgiveness is an expression of spiritual love.

I am human. When I blame others, I avoid taking responsibility. When I forgive others, I show love and compassion.

Today I Am Grateful For:

1.

_____

2.

_____

3.

_____

March 2nd

Morning - Being Flexible and Spiritual

When I am flexible, I am resilient. My spirituality requires more resilience and flexibility. In order for me to be adequately spiritually healthy, I need to be flexible through many of life's challenges. I trust in God's plan for me. I become more flexible and open in my God centered thinking. I grow to become more open to God's love and turn over my negative thoughts and attitudes to God and gain a deeper understanding of who I am. I am flexible. I am resilient.

My Intent For Today:

1.

_____

2.

_____

3.

_____

Evening - Worry to Worship

When I turn worry into worship, God turns my battles into blessings. Worry ends when faith in God begins.

Today I Am Grateful For:

1.

_____

2.

_____

3.

_____

March 3rd

Morning - My Patience
Today I enjoy a deeper level of patience for both myself and for others due to my faith, love and trust in God. God is always patient with me and in turn I grow in my own patience and in my patience towards others.

My Intent For Today:
1.

_____

2.

_____

3.

_____

Evening - Meditation
Through meditation, I look inside me to see what needs to be released. I can remove and release those things that serve me no real purpose.

Today I Am Grateful For:
1.

_____

2.

_____

3.

_____

March 4ᵗʰ

<u>Morning - True Peace</u>
True peace comes when I let God be in control.

My Intent For Today:
1.
_____
2.
_____
3.
_____

<u>Evening - Be Nice, Be Kind</u>
How simple it is to be nice to others, yet how easy it is to hold onto things others do to me that hurt. I try to live my life being kind to all, even those who may not be kind to me. I want to live my life with peace and serenity. This is achieved by being kind to others. If people are not kind to me, I can be kind in my approach to let them know how their actions make me feel. If this does not work, I can kindly walk away from the situation. I will practice being kind in order to maintain my inner peace and protect my serenity.

Today I Am Grateful For:
1.
_____
2.
_____
3.
_____

March 5ᵗʰ

Morning - Change Takes Time

Today I will ask myself: "What is one thing about myself I want to change?" If I give myself an answer readily, I will use today to begin implementing this change. I will do my best to try to implement it. I will not become disappointed or frustrated if the change takes time. What I cannot accomplish today, I can always try for tomorrow.

My Intent For Today:

1.

_____

2.

_____

3.

_____

Evening - Inner Peace

Inner peace requires maintenance. No matter where I am, or what situation I find myself in, peace is always available to me. Peace is a sensation free of conflict or turmoil. If I have moments today when I am not feeling at peace, I will take a few deep breaths. I will hit the pause 🐾 button. I will whisper to myself: "Peace, be still." I affirm that God is present where I am, guiding me to the best outcome for me that only God knows.

Today I Am Grateful For:

1.

_____

2.

_____

3.

_____

March 6ᵗʰ

Morning - God Decides the Weather

God decides the weather for me on any given day. This is a simple thought. God is my forecaster. I truly understand how God has a plan for me. I need the sun … when God decides. I need the rain … when God decides. I need the snow … when God decides. I need the fog … when God decides. Sun provides warmth, rain helps with the harvests, snow can provide snow days and days of family togetherness and fun, which are God's way of forcing me to take rest. On very foggy days when I cannot see clearly, God asks me to trust Him/Her blindly. If I equate this to my own life, I can truly trust in God's plan for my life's journey.

My Intent For Today:

1.

_____

2.

_____

3.

_____

Evening - Home Improvement

I am trying to improve on who I was yesterday. I will use who I am today to be an even better version of me tomorrow. Since my body is my home, I practice home improvement.

Today I Am Grateful For:

1.

_____

2.

_____

3.

_____

March 7th

Morning - Bottling up Emotions

I am an active participant in my emotions and it is up to me to express them all in a way that is healthiest for me. This helps me validate and feel all my feelings and not bottle them up. Bottling up emotions serves me no good purpose. It actually can lead me to having both emotional and/or physical pain. A jar of strawberry preserves can be difficult to open, but once it is opened, it is so worth it.

My Intent For Today:

1.

_____

2.

_____

3.

_____

Evening - I Pray ...

Dear God, tonight I pray for my friends. You know their needs like no one else knows. You know the ones that have secret pain, worries and fears. You are even aware of the loneliness some are feeling right now. I pray You comfort them everywhere they hurt. Refill them with Your love and strength, and restore their hope as they sleep tonight.

Today I Am Grateful For:

1.

_____

2.

_____

3.

_____

March 8th

Morning - God has the Answer
Trust in God's timing.
Rely on God's promises.
Wait for God's answers.
Rejoice in God's goodness.
Believe in God's miracles.
Relax in God's presence.

My Intent For Today:
1.

2.

3.

Evening - My Care, My Heart
When I put my care in God's Hand, God puts His/Her peace in my heart.

Today I Am Grateful For:
1.

2.

3.

March 9th

Morning - Let God do the Rest
When my heart starts to worry, and my mind just cannot rest, I put my prayers down on paper, and let God do the rest.

My Intent For Today:
1.

2.

3.

Evening - Sleep Peacefully
Tonight, I give it to God and sleep peacefully. By keeping it to myself, I may lose sleep.

Today I Am Grateful For:
1.

2.

3.

March 10ᵗʰ

Morning - Accepting Where My Day Takes Me

Today I will focus on accepting what I cannot change and changing what I cannot accept. Today I will accept where my day leads me. I know that God has planned this day especially for me, exactly the way it needs to be for me. I may have plans and yet I accept that I may need to adjust them as my day unfolds. I realize in this adjustment God has planned a day that is unfolding the way it needs to. Today I will accept the unexpected, the plans that may not be my plans ~ because God always has the best plan for ME!

My Intent For Today:

1.

_____

2.

_____

3.

_____

Evening - God's Plan

God's plan is bigger than my mistakes.

Today I Am Grateful For:

1.

_____

2.

_____

3.

_____

March 11ᵗʰ

Morning - Today, I Choose ...

Today I choose God.
Today I choose happiness.
Today I choose peace.
Today I choose love.
Today I choose serenity.
Today I choose kindness.
Today I choose faith.
Today I choose belief.
Today I choose hope.
Today I choose to be the best me I can be.

My Intent For Today:

1.

_____

2.

_____

3.

_____

Evening - I Am a Warrior

Tonight I will be a warrior, not a worrier!

Today I Am Grateful For:

1.

_____

2.

_____

3.

_____

March 12ᵗʰ

<u>Morning - God as My Parent</u>
Good morning My child,
I will handle your life today. Trust ME and walk with ME in faith.
Sit back, relax, and enjoy this day.
Love,
God

My Intent For Today:
1.

_____

2.

_____

3.

_____

<u>Evening - Prayer and Meditation</u>
Prayer washes worry away.
Meditation melts my mindless negative thoughts away.
Through prayer and meditation I am able to clean my mind of all the
dirt that can accumulate.

Today I Am Grateful For:
1.

_____

2.

_____

3.

_____

March 13ᵗʰ

Morning - God as Provider

God is my provider. I shall not worry.

God is the best healthcare provider on the planet. God provides physical, emotional, and spiritual health to me. It does not cost much to let God be my healthcare provider.

My Intent For Today:

1.

_____

2.

_____

3.

_____

Evening - God is High

Never look down on anyone; only God sits that high.

Release judgments and let God be the reason why.

Today I Am Grateful For:

1.

_____

2.

_____

3.

_____

March 14th

Morning - Faith and Control
Faith is having the courage to let God have control.

My Intent For Today:
1.

_____

2.

_____

3.

_____

Evening - Gratitude ...
Gratitude can change my attitude, my reaction, my ability to cope, and my overall outlook on life in the moment. Gratitude sparks goodness, love, kindness, acceptance and compassion.
Gratitude:
1) Monumentally shifts my focus and breathes POSITIVITY
2) Improves my quality of LIFE
3) Increases my happiness
4) Reduces my fears, concerns, resentments, worries and stresses
5) Strengthens my faith
6) Gives me peace of mind
7) Leads me to God
8) Keeps me on my spiritual path

Today I Am Grateful For:
1.

_____

2.

_____

3.

_____

March 15th

Morning - God's Answers to My Prayers

God has one of three answers to my prayers:
1) Yes
2) Not yet
3) I have something better in mind

God answers my prayers in His/Her time, not mine.

My Intent For Today:
1.

_____

2.

_____

3.

_____

Evening - Think ~ Be ~ Trust

Think less
Be faithful
Trust in God

Today I Am Grateful For:
1.

_____

2.

_____

3.

_____

March 16th

Morning - Trust in God

When I cannot, God can.
God's plans are better than my dreams.
I take a deep breath and trust in God.

My Intent For Today:

1.

_____

2.

_____

3.

_____

Evening - Seven Days in a Week

Without God, my week would be:	With God, my week IS:
Sadday	Serene Sunday
Mournday	Meditative Monday
Tearsday	Tranquil Tuesday
Worryday	Wise Wednesday
Thirstday	Thankful Thursday
Fearday	Faithful Friday
Shoutday	Spirited Saturday
7 days without God, makes me weak!	7 days with God, makes me worthy!

Today I Am Grateful For:

1.

_____

2.

_____

3.

_____

March 17th

Morning - Serenity ~ Courage ~ Wisdom

God, for today grant me the serenity to stop beating myself up for not doing things perfectly, the courage to forgive myself because I am working on doing better, and the wisdom to know that You love me just the way I am. Amen.

My Intent For Today:

1.

_____

2.

_____

3.

_____

Evening - Health and Positivity

Healthy positive thoughts will lead me to healthy positive actions and deeds.

Today I Am Grateful For:

1.

_____

2.

_____

3.

_____

March 18ᵗʰ

Morning - Hug Coupon

A hug is the simplest way to tell someone I love them without saying a word. The best thing about a hug, is in order to get one, I have to give one, and vice versa.

Hugs are fat-free, sugar-free and require no batteries. Hugs reduce blood pressure, body temperature and the heart rate. They also relieve pain and depression. They never expire.

HUGS mean:

Hope
Understanding
Gratitude
Serenity

My Intent For Today:

1.

_____

2.

_____

3.

_____

Evening - God's Sky

Today, as I looked up at the beautiful sky, I was in awe of the many shades of blue and the different shapes and consistencies of the clouds. God created all of this for me to contemplate and enjoy. Traveling by airplane is a way to appreciate the Earth's beauty. I peak out my tiny window to see the large landscapes and feel even closer to God so high in the sky.

Today I Am Grateful For:

1.

_____

2.

_____

3.

_____

March 19th

Morning - Concept of Full-Breath Prayers

Focusing on my breath and breathing rhythms brings me calmness and serenity. I am then able to say a sentence or prayer in one full breath and then exhale, which sends this thought/prayer to God in a very special way. Full-breath prayers are powerful, uplifting, and they bring me closer to God. "I pray for those who need Your Love, God" or "I trust in Your plans for me always," are examples.

My Intent For Today:

1.

_____

2.

_____

3.

_____

Evening - Clean Air, Clear Mind and Heart

Breathing in clean air makes my mind fresher and relieves the pressure of my anxiety.
In order to have a clear mind and an open heart, I have to open my mind and clear my heart.

Today I Am Grateful For:

1.

_____

2.

_____

3.

_____

March 20th

Morning - Faith

My faith keeps me spiritually healthy. My faith nourishes my heart and soul, the way the oxygen in the air nourishes my body. My faith lives in the innermost part of my being. Without faith, I am nothing. My faith keeps me strong, even if I feel weak. My faith provides me guidance, when I may feel lost. My faith helps me see the light when there is darkness around me. Faith to me is more than a belief or hope. Faith is the foundation of my spiritual connection to God. My faith keeps me not only centered, but also balanced. My faith keeps my stress, anxiety and fear at bay.

My Intent For Today:

1.

_____

2.

_____

3.

_____

Evening - The Feelings and Attitudes

Tonight, I focus on myself and my feelings to make sure I am healthy and happy. If I feel something is not right, I work at adjusting myself, not at fixing the situation. Sometimes by fixing and adjusting my attitude, the situation appears different to me. This is only because I am in a better space due to an attitude adjustment. It sounds so simple, and it is if I continuously work at it.

Today I Am Grateful For:

1.

_____

2.

_____

3.

_____

March 21st

Morning - Living Life

How one drives a car can say a great deal about how they live their life. If someone is rash in driving, they may be rash or impulsive in their thinking. If someone is overly cautious when driving, they may have difficulty making decisions. If they choose not to use the signal indicator when driving, they may be the type of person that simply expects others to know what is on their mind. If someone keeps switching lanes while driving, they may be a person who has trouble staying focused. Our driving skills truly are a good reflection of how we live our lives. Today I will try to focus on how I drive so I can see how I may be living my life. Drive safe and live safe.

My Intent For Today:
1.

_____

2.

_____

3.

_____

Evening - Trust the Person Who Can ...

I look to trust the person in my life who can see:
The love even though I am angry
The sorrow through my smile
The reason behind my silence
God bless me and allow me to have a great evening knowing that this person is ME.

Today I Am Grateful For:
1.

_____

2.

_____

3.

_____

March 22nd

Morning - The Gift of Love

Today the gift I give myself is to LOVE myself first, and to Love God the way God loves me: UNCONDITIONALLY and ALWAYS.

My Intent For Today:

1.

_____

2.

_____

3.

_____

Evening - When There is No Fear, God is Here

Some people have a fear of flying or an anxiety that develops when flying. Perhaps this is due to not being in control. I myself try to realize that God is always in control and this realization takes the pressure off me. It helps me feel reassured that God always has a plan for me. God is the pilot of all my flights. God is the driver on all my road trips. God is with me on all my walks. God is always in my life and I trust God without any reservation. I am happy to be a passenger with God in the pilot's seat. Today I feel comfortable knowing that God is always in control. God makes my journey a smoother ride.

Today I Am Grateful For:

1.

_____

2.

_____

3.

_____

March 23rd

Morning - The Meanings of Stop

Stop	Stay Calm	Short	Strength	Spirituality
Take a Breath	Think	Time	To	Truly
Observe	Observe	Of	Overcome	Offers
Proceed	Plan	Prayer	Pressure	Peace

My Intent For Today:

1.

_____

2.

_____

3.

_____

Evening - God's Weather

Heavy rains and thunder on a hot summer day provide many signs for me. The heavy rain cools off the summer heat and can symbolize God's shower of love upon each of God's children. The thunder can be God's way of letting me know God is always here. Sometimes the thunder is louder and more frequent. Perhaps God has the need to remind me at certain times more than others. I will enjoy the heavy rain and thunder and feel and hear God's presence all around me, knowing God is showering me with love always.

Today I Am Grateful For:

1.

_____

2.

_____

3.

_____

March 24ᵗʰ

Morning - God Can Handle It All

I can get angry at God. God can handle it. I can take my problems to God. God can take care of them in the way that God knows best. I can share my fears and tears with God. God will turn my fears to faith, and take my tears and save them for another time. God can bear my pain when I feel my pain is too much to bear. It is also important for me to bring my joys and happiness to God and give thanks. God is always planning the best for me. I owe it to myself and God, my Creator, to bring gratitude and not attitude to God. By doing this I become closer to my Creator and feel God's love.

My Intent For Today:

1.

_____

2.

_____

3.

_____

Evening - Trying My Best

Tonight I will try to be my best, do my best and think my best. My best is simply my best, not anyone else's.

Today I Am Grateful For:

1.

_____

2.

_____

3.

_____

March 25ᵗʰ

Morning - God's Gifts to Me

There are many ways to look at nature and truly observe the simple gifts God has given me that I may take for granted. It is important for me to take a few minutes each day to examine the beauty of my natural surroundings. I appreciate how each day that God provides me carries a message, even in the weather. The cool breeze on a hot summer day is God's way of letting me feel God's gentle presence. A white butterfly appearing near me may symbolize a loved one whose spirit is still with me even though they are in Heaven. A bird chirping may be God's song of love to me. Everywhere I look I can see signs, hear sounds, and feel my Creator's presence and love for me. I must be open with my heart, mind and eyes to truly experience it. Today, I will try my best to be open with my heart, mind and eyes, the way God is always open to my love, my pain, my joy, my sorrow, my happiness, and my every emotion.

My Intent For Today:

1.

_____

2.

_____

3.

_____

Evening - Take Better Care of Myself

Tonight I will be extra kind and gentle with myself. I will be compassionate with myself. I will love myself. I will take better care of myself, knowing that by doing so I will be better able to take care of those that may need my care.

Today I Am Grateful For:

1.

_____

2.

_____

3.

_____

March 26th

Morning - Keeping the Focus

The true success of fulfilling my dreams comes from me trying my best. My effort is what God sees. When I fail or endure difficult times in my life, it is God who is there watching over me, walking by my side, keeping me safe always. No one promised me at my birth that life would be easy, simple or without trouble. It is up to me to keep the focus on what is truly important and to always keep God with me even when I may be upset with God or when I am not in sync with God's plan for me.

My Intent For Today:

1.

_____

2.

_____

3.

_____

Evening - Be Kind and Gentle

How can I fix something I did not cause? All I can do is make sure I contribute to any situation in a healthy way. I try daily to be kind and gentle with myself.

When I live in fear, I foolishly rely on my power and NOT my Higher Power.

Today I Am Grateful For:

1.

_____

2.

_____

3.

_____

March 27th

Morning - God Loves ♡ Me

There are days when I feel so accomplished and then there are days that I wish I could start all over again. The lesson here is for me to be okay with having both kinds of days. I am not a perfect being. I am perfect at being human. Like all humans, I have my faults, my good traits, and I am flawed. Yet I know that God loves me—flaws and all. We humans are beautiful with our flaws like a rose bush with thorns. I take solace in knowing that God accepts me and does not judge me.

God loves me, with my flaws and all.
Break me, mold me, make me.

My Intent For Today:
1.

_____

2.

_____

3.

_____

Evening - Accepting the Unexpected

Tonight I will focus on accepting what I cannot change and changing what I feel I can. It may be very difficult and yet I am willing to try this. I also will learn to accept the unexpected since this too is part of life.

Today I Am Grateful For:
1.

_____

2.

_____

3.

_____

March 28ᵗʰ

Morning - The New Normals

Marriage, birth of children, passing of loved ones, adoption, divorce, and a pandemic are all changes that become new normals for anyone. So new normals can be positive as well as not so positive changes in my life. Today I will try to become open to adjusting to everyday new normals that occur in my life and know that God plans for me better than I could ever do for myself.

My Intent For Today:
1.

_____

2.

_____

3.

_____

Evening - I Walk in Faith with God

Tonight, I remind myself of many things. I will work to improve my strengths and work to diminish my weaknesses. I will walk in faith with God knowing that the steps I take have already been decided by God, for God knows best which path my life will take. I will do my best to smile at all those who cross my path. God has decided whom I will meet along my journey and I trust that those I meet have a purpose in crossing my path. The purpose may be a blessing or may be a lesson. I only need to keep both my mind and heart open to them.

Today I Am Grateful For:
1.

_____

2.

_____

3.

_____

March 29th

Morning - Leave Judgment and Worry to God

Judging others is so unhealthy. It makes me feel like I am saying I am better than the person I am judging, which could not be further from the truth. Similar to how I leave worrying to God, I try to leave judgment of others to God as well. God is much better at both worrying and judging. I have a tough enough job keeping the focus on myself rather than concerning myself with how I feel about what others are or are not doing. I shall do my best today to not pass judgment on anyone—even myself.

My Intent For Today:
1.

_____

2.

_____

3.

_____

Evening - What a Difference a Smile 😃 Makes

A smile 😃 can change not only my outlook, it can also bring a smile to someone else and change their outlook. An act of kindness can bring joy to my life and to the person to whom I am being kind. I will try and perform an act of kindness with a smile on my face and bring joy to myself first and then to others. If I am successful I will do my best to encourage someone else to pay this forward. Spreading positivity and joy to others is a beautiful gesture that does not require too much from me. The rewards are priceless.

Today I Am Grateful For:
1.

_____

2.

_____

3.

_____

March 30ᵗʰ

Morning - Expectations Lead to Frustration

When I really know somebody, I cannot hate them. Or maybe it is just that I cannot really know them until I stop hating them.

EXPECTATIONS – OBSERVATIONS = FRUSTRATIONS

If I let my observations exceed my expectations, I am simply going with the flow.

My Intent For Today:

1.

_____

2.

_____

3.

_____

Evening - God's Got It Covered

When I rely on God for strength, I do not have to be so strong. When I let God worry, I do not have to worry. When I put my trust in God, God guides me onto the right path. When I fall, God is right there to pick me up. When I make mistakes, God does not judge me, instead God loves me more. God forgives me when I cannot forgive myself. God has it all covered, so I simply need to turn it all over and God will handle what I cannot. God's got this when I do not!

Today I Am Grateful For:

1.

_____

2.

_____

3.

_____

March 31st

Morning - I Am Feeling Great!
Today I wake up feeling **GREAT**!

GREAT today means:
Getting
Really
Excited
About
Today

I will practice mindfulness even more today. When I brush my teeth, I will focus on each tooth with care the way my hygienist does during my teeth cleaning. When I apply face cream, I will apply it with the same care an aesthetician would. When I get dressed, I will dress my best. When I speak with others today, I will try my best to speak with utmost kindness. Today I will work at being **GREAT!**

My Intent For Today:
1.

2.

3.

Evening - The Courage in My Soul
I have so much courage in my soul, and this is from learning to relinquish my control.

Today I Am Grateful For:
1.

2.

3.

APRIL

ACCEPTANCE

April 1st

Morning - What Family Means to Me
FAMILY means:

Friends	Faith
And	And
Mentors	Meditation
I	Inspires
Love	Loving
You	Yourself

My Intent For Today:
1.

_____

2.

_____

3.

_____

Evening - My Pilot Light
I believe I have a pilot light inside me that is always lit. It is there to be increased into a higher flame that will heighten my spiritual growth and bring me closer to God's love.

Today I Am Grateful For:
1.

_____

2.

_____

3.

_____

April 2ⁿᵈ

Morning - Love, Support and Celebration
To love is not fixing, it is supporting.
Love is letting it begin with ME.
Love life, live life and celebrate today.

My Intent For Today:
1.

_____

2.

_____

3.

_____

Evening - What is Shame?
SHAME may mean:

Suffering	**S**hould
Has	**H**ave
A	**A**lready
Measured	**M**astered
Effect	**E**verything

Today I Am Grateful For:
1.

_____

2.

_____

3.

_____

April 3rd

Morning - Taking a Paws

PAWS means:
Praying or **P**ausing
Always
Works
Strongly

My Intent For Today:

1.

_____

2.

_____

3.

_____

Evening - Detachment is ...

Detachment means a change in my relationship behaviors. It can also mean making amends. Detachment is also about setting healthy personal boundaries that are NOT etched in stone and can change as I change.

Today I Am Grateful For:

1.

_____

2.

_____

3.

_____

April 4th

Morning - What is Truth?

TRUTH means:

Taking	**T**o
Real	**R**ealize
Understanding	**U**r
To	**T**ruly
Heart	**H**elpful

My Intent For Today:

1.

2.

3.

Evening - All About God

God's Plan is Perfect!
God has the best GPS. Turn it on.
Am I journeying daily with God?

Today I Am Grateful For:

1.

2.

3.

April 5th

Morning - Acceptance

Today I will accept where my day leads me. I know that God has planned this day especially for me, exactly the way it needs to be for me. I may have my plans set and yet I accept that I may need to adjust them as my day unfolds. I realize that in the adjustment, God has planned a day that is unfolding exactly the way it needs to. Today I will accept the unexpected, the plans that may not be my plans - because God always has the best plan for ME! There is my plan and there is the right plan —> God's plan.

My Intent For Today:

1.

_____

2.

_____

3.

_____

Evening - Help versus Hope

HELP means:		**HOPE** means:	
His/Her	Hope	Hearing	Hang
Ever	Encouragement	Other	On
Loving	Love	People's	Peace
Presence	Patience	Experiences	Exists

Today I Am Grateful For:

1.

_____

2.

_____

3.

_____

April 6ᵗʰ

Morning - Patience

My thoughts are what lead to my actions. Sometimes my thoughts may not be the best for me. When I feel any hesitation before acting upon my thoughts, I know I can pause 🐾, wait and think about my actions before carrying them out. I am learning to be patient and slow down my thinking. Sometimes slower thinking is actually a good thing, similar to a slow cooker. Good things can happen when I wait. Even in times when my thoughts travel to places in the future, it is best to stay in the current moment and not think about the future, because then I am losing out on the here and now. Today I will pause 🐾 and wait before acting on my thoughts.

My Intent For Today:

1.

_____

2.

_____

3.

_____

Evening - Am I Willing?

When
I
Live
Life
I
Need
God

Tonight, I am becoming more willing.

Today I Am Grateful For:

1.

_____

2.

_____

3.

_____

April 7th

Morning - Peace

When I strive for peace with others, I must be at peace within first. When my focus is to help someone else, I have to make sure I am healthy first. If I feel anything but healthy and peaceful inside, I am probably not at my best to promote health and peace with others. This acceptance allows me to take a step back and readjust, recharge myself before I attempt to be there for another person. If I can acknowledge this for myself first, I am likely to become a better version of ME!

My Intent For Today:

1.

_____

2.

_____

3.

_____

Evening - Action

ACTION means:

Any
Changes
Towards
Improving
One's
Nature

Today I Am Grateful For:

1.

_____

2.

_____

3.

_____

April 8ᵗʰ

Morning - Choices

Each moment today is a chance to start the next phase of my life's journey. The choices I make are subject to change, because I am changing also. Who I am today is a reflection of the people in my life whom I value and who have influenced my life. Today I will make choices to be around people with similar values. I will keep my mind open to learn from all the people I meet today and all the circumstances I go through. Learning through life's experiences is a continual process and because each of us is different, our learning experiences are different. Today I will be open to all that I learn.

My Intent For Today:

1.

_____

2.

_____

3.

_____

Evening - God's Program:

PROGRAM means:

People
Relying
On
God
Relaying
A
Message

Tonight, I will trust in having a **PROGRAM**. God's Program for me.

Today I Am Grateful For:

1.

_____

2.

_____

3.

_____

April 9th

Morning - Past Feelings

Sometimes my mind goes back into the past and uses the past to project what may happen in the future. When this happens I allow myself a few minutes to pause 🐾. I ask myself, "Why am I feeling this way?" "What good can come from this?" Usually by doing this small exercise, I find myself realizing that my feelings and thoughts are not serving me well, and I think of something I am grateful for. By doing this, my thoughts become positive and healthy. This usually leads me to positive actions. Today I will practice this exercise more in order to push through the unhealthy feelings and thoughts, and focus on gratitude.

My Intent For Today:

1.

_____

2.

_____

3.

_____

Evening - Pace

PACE means:

Positive	**P**ausing	**P**raying
Attitudes	**A**llows	**A**lways
Change	**C**reative	**C**hanges
Everything	**E**nergy	**E**verything

Today I Am Grateful For:

1.

_____

2.

_____

3.

_____

April 10th

Morning - Struggle and Comfort

Life may feel like a struggle at times. The beautiful thing to remember is that there is life. Staying in the moment keeps me healthy. Today I will do my best to enjoy life which means enduring the struggles as well. I will also remind myself that God is always there to enjoy my life and help me through the struggles. I feel very comforted knowing that I am not alone and that God travels with me throughout my life's journey.

My Intent For Today:

1.

_____

2.

_____

3.

_____

Evening - Faith

When a day comes to completion, I thank God for the day. I am grateful for getting through it if it was a difficult day, and I am even more grateful if it was a peaceful day. Each day brings its own uniqueness to my journey. I measure my faith by all the moments where I turn to God, the happy ones and the ones that I need more help coping with. I remember that God is always there with me. God loves me unconditionally and knows what is best for me at all times.

Today I Am Grateful For:

1.

_____

2.

_____

3.

_____

April 11ᵗʰ

Morning - Health

It is important to stay healthy in every way: physically, mentally, emotionally, spiritually and financially. I will do my best to focus on my health today in all five facets and keep them in balance. I can keep these five facets of my health connected in my one hand ✋.

My Intent For Today:

1.

_____

2.

_____

3.

_____

Evening - Moderation

Everything in today's world is moving too fast and this is not necessarily the best pace for me. Doing things fast can lead to mistakes. When I take my time, I can actually stay calm. There are times/situations when I need to do things fast, but it is NOT often. When I meditate, I take slow deep breaths to bring more calmness into my inner being. When I play tennis, yes, I run fast as needed, but not all the time. Most of the things I need to do, I can do at a moderate pace which keeps me balanced. Tonight I will practice staying at a moderate pace which is much healthier for me. The more I practice this, the more it becomes part of my daily routine.

Today I Am Grateful For:

1.

_____

2.

_____

3.

_____

April 12th

Morning - Mistakes

Being human, I am flawed and God loves me anyway. I make mistakes and God loves me anyway. I ask for things I may not need and God loves me anyway. I get angry at God and God loves me anyway. I thank God for the blessings I have. I may not always remember God but God loves me anyway. The beautiful thing is God is the ONE BEING I can always count on. God loves me unconditionally. It may be best to trust in this, appreciate this, and love God the way God loves me. I say "Good morning, God"; "Thank You, God"; "I love You, God"; and "Good night, God" daily. Today I will practice this more and feel God's love, hugs and energy throughout my day. Thank God for God.

My Intent For Today:

1.

_____

2.

_____

3.

_____

Evening - Time

Time stands still when I let my mind stand still. When my heart is at rest, it helps my mind to rest. This is a time when I become my best. When I look out at the water at the beach and watch the gentleness of the waves touching the sand, I am reminded to slow my thinking down, pause and reflect. Then the leaves on the trees sway ever so gently, there is a calmness in the air and the birds chirp softly. I am reminded to enjoy nature and the peace that comes with the stillness. I try to carry this peace with me wherever I go. If I am unable to, this is okay. Nothing is lost because I was able to experience the calmness and peace for a while.

Today I Am Grateful For:

1.

_____

2.

_____

3.

_____

April 13th

Morning - God

God is the reason for all joy in my life. God brings me peace. God helps me see things more clearly. God aids in my hearing things more sincerely. I am forever thankful for God being in my life. I thank God for giving me life. My goal is to show God my thanks for being part of His/Her existence by working at this connection each and every day.

My Intent For Today:

1.

_____

2.

_____

3.

_____

Evening - Change

When I look at photos from my life, I am able to tangibly see how I have changed in height, stature, appearance, etc. I am also able to see how people in my life have grown and changed as well. I am able to see how people have come and gone in my life. I can see how times have changed, fashions have changed, photography has changed. The one constant is change. Life is ever changing and I am ever changing. God loves me through all the changes. All this change is essential to God's plan for me as I am changing. It is all about CHANGE.

Today I Am Grateful For:

1.

_____

2.

_____

3.

_____

April 14th

Morning - Emotions

I experience many difficult emotions at different times: fear, joy, anger, happiness, excitement, sadness, concern, grief, pride, etc. These emotions are directly connected to the life experience or situation I am going through. Being able to express or feel my emotions without someone saying "Do not cry" or "You should be happy" may not happen because my fellow humans often think they know how I feel or how I should feel. Today I will honor my feelings and express them. I will try not to sit in the negative ones for too long. I know that by going through the feelings, I am growing/changing in a way that will help me. I may not understand why at the time and that is alright. My life matters.

My Intent For Today:

1.

2.

3.

Evening - Past

I learn to close the door to my past. I open the door to my future. I take a deep breath and turn to a new page in the book of my life.

Today I Am Grateful For:

1.

2.

3.

April 15th

Morning - Ownership

Ownership and acceptance are two gifts in my life I may take for granted. Owning my actions and accepting things I cannot change are essential to keeping me healthy. Often I focus on the negative too much and forget the positive. To keep the balance, for each negative thing I must push a positive one in front of me. This keeps the balance. Relaxing my mind is essential. Changing myself through both my thoughts and actions is an extremely healthy way to live a good life. Today I will practice all of the above. Love is a beautiful way to start. The more I try, the better I become.

My Intent For Today:

1.

2.

3.

Evening - Prayer and Positivity

The power of prayer with positive thoughts and energy is a beautiful thing. Sending out positive energy to others comes from practicing positive thoughts and positive actions. It is a simple act of kindness I can share with others. I can share it with strangers and thus it becomes a random act of kindness. What a beautiful thing to do daily. Some days I challenge myself more by trying to do at least three random acts of kindness. I do not get disheartened if I cannot accomplish the three, because the idea of trying is a beautiful gift.

Today I Am Grateful For:

1.

2.

3.

April 16th

Morning - Change

If I want to see how the world sees me, I take a look in the mirror. If I do not like what I see, I have the power to change this. I change it and take a look in the mirror again and I will show the world what I now see. If I want to hear how I sound to others, I make a voice memo and play it back to myself so I can hear myself. If I do not like how I sound, I have the power to change it. I can re-record the voice memo, replay it and if I now like it, this is how I want to sound. Today I will practice this simple exercise and change to become a better version of me both in appearance and sound. The changes I make are changes I want to make.

My Intent For Today:

1.

_____

2.

_____

3.

_____

Evening - Life

I equate living life to an ice cream sundae ... I choose the flavors of ice cream. I choose the toppings. I enjoy all of it, because I choose to!

Today I Am Grateful For:

1.

_____

2.

_____

3.

_____

April 17th

Morning - Dear God

I said a prayer for you today that God will touch you with His healing Hand and give you the comfort and peace you need to get through. Dear God, please wrap Your loving arms around those who are hurting today and let them feel how much You truly love them.

Love gives me Hope. Hope builds Faith. Faith brings me closer to God. I keep loving, keep hoping, and always have faith in God.

Dear God, I pray that my family may always live in peace. May we understand each other, may we have patience, and may we let You know first about every problem we are facing as a family.

My Intent For Today:

1.

_____

2.

_____

3.

_____

Evening - Windshield

I try to look at life through the windshield, not the rearview mirror. I can glance in the rearview mirror and look at my past to learn from it and reference it. Then I come back to the present, which is truly a gift.

Today I Am Grateful For:

1.

_____

2.

_____

3.

_____

April 18ᵗʰ

Morning - Pilot Light of Serenity

The pilot light of my serenity and inner happiness is always burning bright inside of me. I am in control of increasing the flame which heightens my serenity and inner happiness by simply turning inward, feeling the warmth, and then sharing it outwardly with others.

My Intent For Today:

1.

_____

2.

_____

3.

_____

Evening - Hugs

When I receive many hugs and give many hugs, it is a win-win. As in tennis, the score would be love-all with hugs.

Today I Am Grateful For:

1.

_____

2.

_____

3.

_____

April 19th

Morning - Change

The best way for me to improve my life is by me changing in a positive way. By embracing the desire to change, I take the first steps to amend my life. Amendments are simply additions or deletions I make to who I basically am.

My Intent For Today:

1.

_____

2.

_____

3.

_____

Evening - Connection with God

To reach my full potential, which is infinite, it is very important for me to strengthen my connection to God. God always knows my potential and has unconditional faith, trust and love in me. By increasing my spiritual connection, I increase my value. I will work on continuing to fire up my spiritual connection and watch amazing things about me unfold. As a flower blooms, so am I continuously blooming with God watering me with love. With every rainfall, God showers me with love.

Today I Am Grateful For:

1.

_____

2.

_____

3.

_____

April 20th

Morning - Balance

Work is a beautiful thing when done in moderation. Everything in moderation is healthy. Too much of anything disrupts the balance. Today I will try to stay balanced and not get upset if I am unable to maintain my balance.

My Intent For Today:

1.

_____

2.

_____

3.

_____

Evening - Time

Taking my time to walk through life is both very important and healthy to me. Rushing often causes poor decisions. Tonight I will take my time walking through the rest of the evening.

Today I Am Grateful For:

1.

_____

2.

_____

3.

_____

April 21ˢᵗ

Morning - Love
Feeling the love I give is just as important as feeling the love I receive.

My Intent For Today:
1.

_____

2.

_____

3.

_____

Evening - Acceptance
Accepting situations and accepting people has become easier for me because I want others to be accepting of me. I too have my quirks and certainly can be "off" at any given moment on any given day. I focus on knowing that it is okay dealing with people who are not on the same page as me as long as I can achieve the results that keep me comfortable, safe, and do not cause me stress. If I am uncomfortable, unsafe, or stressed, I need to be able to focus on my physical health, bring calmness to my soul and carry on with the issue at hand. When I am honest with how I am feeling, I am better able to handle any situation.

Today I Am Grateful For:
1.

_____

2.

_____

3.

_____

April 22nd

Morning - Listening

When I am feeling uncomfortable about something, whether it be physical or emotional, it helps me to take a pause 🐾, give myself the respect of acknowledging my discomfort and realize that listening to myself is a very good thing. This is a GIFT I can give myself. Today I will listen to myself more.

My Intent For Today:

1.

2.

3.

Evening - Weathering the Storm

Storms, wind, rain and extreme sun all have an effect on me. My mood can be affected by the weather. It takes strength to weather a storm and the good news is that I am not alone ... ever. God is helping me weather the storm. God is also with me when the sun shines brightly upon my face. I am extremely blessed to have God always traveling on my journey as the tour guide. Sometimes I do not listen to the guide and stray away from the tour and go off on my own. This does not always work out well for me. Staying on the tour and listening to the Master Tour Guide ... aka God ... is always a good thing for me and results in my following God's plan. I will do my best to stay on the tour and listen to the Master Tour Guide ... God.

Today I Am Grateful For:

1.

2.

3.

April 23rd

Morning - Accountability

The way I walk through my life is a reflection of my behavior and my actions. I am accountable for how I speak, act, observe, listen and move. It is important for me to want to improve my actions. I can do this by learning from my past. I will work on my actions and how they affect me as I walk through my life. My past can help me with my future and I choose to keep an open mind as I walk through life. I will walk slowly and enjoy my life fully.

My Intent For Today:

1.

_____

2.

_____

3.

_____

Evening - Growth

Specific dates and times from my past help me remember where I was and what I was doing when events happened. These dates and times serve as references for me. Some of these references are essential to my personal growth and spiritual development. They can be very helpful as reminders of how much I have already grown and how much growth I still need to accomplish. I will never forget, will always remember, and hopefully will become stronger.

Today I Am Grateful For:

1.

_____

2.

_____

3.

_____

April 24th

Morning - Forgiveness

Forgiveness is a gift I give to myself. When I practice forgiveness, I feel healthier. It is an act that helps me stay healthy. I can start simply by thinking of whom I need to forgive and send some positive energy that person's way. Once I do this, I can move forward with my own life. God helps me with this. God always forgives me when I am not at my best—the best that God knows I can be. The best way to start forgiving is to forgive myself for not being able to forgive others, YET!

My Intent For Today:

1.

2.

3.

Evening - Strength

My challenges and my struggles are what made me a healthier, stronger person. They bring me closer to my faith. Knowing that God is with me through the joys and struggles of life truly gives me serenity.

Today I Am Grateful For:

1.

2.

3.

April 25th

Morning - Positivity

Each new day that I awake is a gift; a new chance; a new opportunity to better myself. I am able to make yesterday's changes. I am able to see how much I want to grow and I grasp the opportunity to do so. If I am unable to institute changes due to circumstances beyond my control, I will accept this and know that I can try again. God is on my side and knows my intention is there. Today I take the opportunity to institute positive changes that shape me into a better version of me.

My Intent For Today:

1.

2.

3.

Evening - God

Wherever I am, whatever I do, whomever I am with, whenever it is ... God is always with me. Sometimes I forget this simple concept: God is there for me, to catch me when I fall, to love and support me always. I as a human can get caught up in thinking I know what to do at all times. Each day, I am learning something new not only about myself, but also about life in general. I try to keep both my mind and heart open to these new discoveries and move forward in my life, deepening my connection with God.

Today I Am Grateful For:

1.

2.

3.

April 26th

Morning - Health

My health is vitally important to me. This means my physical, mental, emotional, financial and spiritual health. Being healthy deepens every part of me. Today I will do my best to stay healthy!

My Intent For Today:

1.

_____

2.

_____

3.

_____

Evening - Meditation

There are nights when my sleep may be disrupted, or I may have trouble falling asleep. I am learning that these are moments for me to expand my connection with God by prayer, meditation, and self-reflection. I am able to use this time to converse with God and simply listen/look for signals from God. By letting God guide me and turning myself over to faith, trust and love in God, I often am able to fall back to sleep. Today I will utilize the tools I have to expand my spiritual connection with God, especially in moments when I have trouble sleeping. God loves me always and does not mind me bringing myself closer to Him/Her even in times of sleeplessness.

Today I Am Grateful For:

1.

_____

2.

_____

3.

_____

April 27th

Morning - Emotions

My thoughts and feelings are important in allowing me to either stay in the moment or move forward. Negative thoughts and feelings can cause me more harm physically, emotionally and spiritually. It is important for me to feel my feelings in order to heal and move forward. If I push away or bury my negative emotions, I do not allow myself the opportunity for growth from painful experiences. Today I will try to feel my pain, experience it, learn and grow from it. I know that by doing this there will be many benefits that I may not completely understand right now, but I will in time ... God's time.

My Intent For Today:

1.

_____

2.

_____

3.

_____

Evening - Grief

Grief is unexpressed love for the loved one lost. I can take the unexpressed love and share this love with another person. This expression of love is a way of releasing the sadness of my grief, in other words, a way of coping with my loss.

Today I Am Grateful For:

1.

_____

2.

_____

3.

_____

April 28th

Morning - One Day at a Time

Each new day is a clean slate for me. It is divided into three parts—morning, afternoon and evening—for reasons. If the morning gets off to a good start, this is wonderful. If the morning does not, I can use the afternoon to begin anew. If the morning is good, and the afternoon is not so good, and the evening is worse, I realize the morning part was still good. I can focus on the good parts and learn from the not so good. If the day in its three parts ebbs and flows well, then that truly simulates life. And so this day is truly a gift. Today I will simply see how the three parts of my day go and enjoy.

My Intent For Today:

1.

2.

3.

Evening - The Challenge of Kindness

Being kind to people is a beautiful thing. The MOST rewarding challenge is to be kind to unkind people. The SUPER rewarding experience is to go a full day without criticizing anyone … including myself.

Today I Am Grateful For:

1.

2.

3.

April 29th

Morning - Calm

When I have a day where it seems like things just keep going wrong, I take a pause , take a break from my day, take a walk or simply take some deep breaths. When I regain my calmness, I resume my day with some newfound energy. Every day is not going to be good and this is okay. When I have a day that goes relatively smoothly or well, I can appreciate it even more. I can use the good day as a reference point for the next not-so-good one.

My Intent For Today:

1.

_____

2.

_____

3.

_____

Evening - Tools

I am a beautiful human created by God. God has even put some of Him/Her in me so I can feel God with me at all times. During moments of difficulty or stress, I remind myself of God being in me and it warms my heart. I also remember that when I smile, my pilot light of happiness gets brighter and stronger. These are essential tools that keep my serenity, peace and calmness strong. I will use my tools as needed.

Today I Am Grateful For:

1.

_____

2.

_____

3.

_____

April 30th

Morning - Happiness

If only I could select my thoughts/moods for the day the way I select the outfit I choose to wear for the day ...

Hmm ...

Today I will do my best to remind myself that my happiness is in my control as is my peace. I imagine two small dials on either earlobe: one is my peace dial, the other is my happiness dial. I simply adjust the dials as needed throughout my day. A gentle touch on the back of my lower earlobe can adjust either my happiness or peace depending on which needs more adjusting. It is a simple concept to keep my happiness and peace in my control, as it needs to be.

My Intent For Today:
1.

_____

2.

_____

3.

_____

Evening - Time and Self Care

Multitasking is very unhealthy for me. Although I may have done things all at once in the past, does not mean I want to do them that way now. I have grown and I am learning healthier ways to do my tasks calmly, peacefully, one step at a time. I am being smart and healthy about how I handle my obligations. I am learning to RELAX and ENJOY ME!

Today I Am Grateful For:
1.

_____

2.

_____

3.

_____

MAY

HAPPINESS

May 1st

Morning - Life

God determined the day and time I would make my appearance on Earth and to whom I would belong. God has also decided when I will return home to Heaven, on which day and at what time. All the time in between is open and up to me to enjoy, to appreciate, and to leave my mark on all those whom I meet.

My Intent For Today:

1.
_____

2.
_____

3.
_____

Evening - Relax

When I am under immense pressure or stress either at work or in my family life, there are tools I use to help me bring the focus back to me. This brings calmness, peace and serenity to my physical, emotional and spiritual being. My technique involves the word, **RELAX**:

Recognize = Recognizing I have stress
is the first step to managing my stress

Exercise = Exercising to deviate and release my negative emotions

Letting go = Letting go of things not in my control

Attitude = Keeping my attitude positive and
healthy. Steering clear of negativity

Xtra Sleep = Sleeping renews and regenerates the body and mind.
Sleep gives me energy and better mental acuity

Today I Am Grateful For:

1.
_____

2.
_____

3.
_____

May 2nd

Morning - Thanking God

Today, I take my time to love God for being with me always. I thank God for caring about me always. I appreciate God for filling my life with faith, love, hope, joy and peace. I feel blessed with God's guidance, support, and unconditional love. Today I will work towards sharing God's love for me with others. Today, I will improve my relationship with God, and delight in knowing how much God works at staying active in my life. God is my biggest supporter and cheerleader. God is my best friend, even when I may not be God's best friend.

My Intent For Today:

1.

2.

3.

Evening - Mature

I will try my best to be **MATURE**:
My
Ability
To
Understand
Removes
Expectations

I become more **MATURE** when I turn to God for suggestions on how to proceed in my life.

Today I Am Grateful For:

1.

2.

3.

May 3rd

Morning - Sadness

There are times when I recall sad memories and I allow myself to feel the sadness for a little while. Then I try to recall a happy memory to offset the sad one. This practice helps me stay balanced. My memories are what they are. They are flashbacks of my experiences. They are part of me—just a part, not the whole. I try to stay in the current moment and if I linger in the past for too long, I remind myself of something I am grateful for or feel blessed about. This exercise also helps me stay positive. Today I will do my best to stay balanced and to stay positive.

My Intent For Today:

1.

2.

3.

Evening - Nature

Nature is meant to be nurtured. When I nurture nature, I show God the love that God shows me. Through this exercise, I learn how to appreciate the simple things in life and to keep simplicity in my life.

Today I Am Grateful For:

1.

2.

3.

May 4ᵗʰ

Morning - Focus

When I keep the focus on me and not concern myself with others, my life is simpler. I need only focus on others when they ask for my input. This simple rule is one that helps keep me healthy and I work less.

My Intent For Today:

1.

_____

2.

_____

3.

_____

Evening - Calmness

Water is like my heart and mind. At times water can be still, serene and calm. At other times, water can be troubled and tumultuous. The waves can be overbearing and cause damage to the things that are nearby. If I remind myself that my mind and heart are like water, and that like water, my mind and heart will have moments of calmness and serenity but also other moments of tumult, trouble, or even chaos. The important thing to remember is that these moments are moments and they do pass. They do not last forever. I will do my best to keep my mind and heart at rest like the calmness of water.

Today I Am Grateful For:

1.

_____

2.

_____

3.

_____

May 5th

Morning - Listening

I want to enjoy listening to others the way I love listening to music. If I can accomplish this, I become more compassionate, loving and respectful of the person I am listening to. They in turn may learn to respect and love me. So it is a win-win simply by me opening my ears more. I have two ears and one mouth, to listen more and talk less.

My Intent For Today:

1.
_____

2.
_____

3.
_____

Evening - Serenity

There are nights when my sleep is interrupted either by noises due to nature ~ rain, thunder, lightning ~ or by my own inability to stay asleep due to an overactive mind. On these nights, I use the time awake to either pray or meditate. I try to be patient with myself and not become frustrated with the sleeplessness, instead being grateful for the opportunity to pray (converse with God) or meditate (listen to God). With the right frame of mind and no expectations, usually I am able to fall back to sleep with a little more peace inside me.

Today I Am Grateful For:

1.
_____

2.
_____

3.
_____

May 6th

<u>Morning - Choices</u>
Today I choose love.
Today I choose happiness.
Today I choose to be a better version of me.
Today I choose living life to the fullest.
Today I choose to be more accepting and do less expecting.
Today I choose to be kind and gentle with myself.
Today I choose to be at peace with who I am.

My Intent For Today:
1.

_____

2.

_____

3.

_____

<u>Evening - Peace</u>
It is possible for me to maintain my peace and serenity even during times of strife and chaos. At these times, I find myself even more proud and grateful for me being me.

Today I Am Grateful For:
1.

_____

2.

_____

3.

_____

May 7th

Morning - Health
Health is five-fold:
>Physical
>>Emotional
>>>Spiritual
>>>>Mental
>>>>>Financial

All five parts are essential to my overall well-being and need to be in balance.
Physical health comes from a deeper connection with my senses ~ all five senses: sight, taste, touch, smell and hearing.
Emotional health comes from a deeper connection and understanding of my feelings.
Spiritual health comes from a deeper connection with God.
Mental health comes from a deeper connection to my mind's muscle.
Financial health comes from a deeper connection to my understanding of how much I need.

My Intent For Today:
1.

_____

2.

_____

3.

_____

Evening - Faith
By opening my mind and heart, by closing my mouth, and by keeping my body moving forward, I reach new levels of faith I never thought I could achieve.

Today I Am Grateful For:
1.

_____

2.

_____

3.

_____

May 8ᵗʰ

Morning - Love

Love is so much more than four letters. Love can mean letting go of something/someone. Love can be a feeling, a thought, or an action. Love can be patience. Love can be kindness extended to a stranger. Love can be simply a HUG shared with someone in need of one. Love can be giving one's time to either oneself or to someone who needs the help. Love can be simply being there for myself or for someone else. All I need is LOVE. Today I will do my best to love more.

My Intent For Today:

1.

_____

2.

_____

3.

_____

Evening - Life is a Puzzle

Life is like a puzzle and sometimes we find other people in our life that fit perfectly. Those are life's best moments.

Today I Am Grateful For:

1.

_____

2.

_____

3.

_____

May 9th

Morning - Sanity

Working on my serenity is my sanity.
My sanity and my serenity are in my hands and I will do my best to hold onto both today.

My Intent For Today:

1.

_____

2.

_____

3.

_____

Evening - Gifts 💝

My life is a gift 💝 and I intend to treasure the gift. This gift is given to me by God. The gift I give to God is to live my life to the fullest tonight and each day after. Each day that I can do this, is a day lived well and I trust that God will give me many more days ahead.

Today I Am Grateful For:

1.

_____

2.

_____

3.

_____

May 10ᵗʰ

Morning - True Self

By being my true self, I learn to live my life without worry of what others think of me. I learn to love and respect myself more and I even grow. I begin to liberate myself and I stop allowing others to have power or control over me. By honoring my true self, I become more comfortable and with time I become more used to this new me. In even more time, those who care and love me, learn to enjoy this new me. I am becoming the me that God intended me to be. This new me makes both God and me very HAPPY.

My Intent For Today:

1.

2.

3.

Evening - Growth

Only now can I understand that my very first relationship was the one I had with my mother while in utero—where I do not recall much, but I probably was able to hear my mum's voice. I could hear my mum's heartbeat and I could probably see her heart from the inside. Only a child can see their mum's heart from the inside. As this in utero baby, I did much more listening, because babies in utero cannot speak. I will do my best to listen more and speak less. I can learn more from listening and through learning, I will grow.

Today I Am Grateful For:

1.

2.

3.

May 11th

Morning - Emotional Awareness

Today I bring awareness to my emotions. My emotions certainly affect my physical body and also my spirit. By focusing on my emotional awareness, I can actually become better at handling and working through my emotions—especially the ones that I have more difficulty with. When I work at maintaining my emotional, physical and spiritual health, I reap the benefits of staying healthy. Just like there are days when I am not physically okay, there are days I am not emotionally okay. On these days, I take extra care to be kind and gentle with myself. My overall health matters and is essential to me living well.

My Intent For Today:

1.

_____

2.

_____

3.

_____

Evening - Serenity

I am learning new things about myself all the time. I am changing and able to work at maintaining my serenity especially during times of extreme stress and extreme joy. Serenity is not simply a state of mind for me. Serenity is a physical thing for me as well. Serenity gives me a protective coat, so to speak, similar to sunscreen which protects me from the harmful things that can destroy my peace.

Today I Am Grateful For:

1.

_____

2.

_____

3.

_____

May 12th

Morning - Love, Trust and Belief

Before I can believe, love and trust in others, I must learn to believe, love and trust myself. Doubting myself never does me any good and usually leads me to unhealthy actions. When doubt and fear creeps into my mind, I work hard at shifting my focus to more positive and healthy thoughts, even memories. Once my thoughts are more positive, I can feel confident that positive actions will soon follow. My awareness of this whole process has developed over time and I continually work at it, because I, being human, can quickly fall back to old, unhealthy thinking patterns if I do not stay alert and aware.

My Intent For Today:

1.

_____

2.

_____

3.

_____

Evening - Serenity

Serenity is a calmness or a state of peace, and can be maintained even in the midst of chaos or crisis.

Today I Am Grateful For:

1.

_____

2.

_____

3.

_____

May 13th

Morning - My Heart and My Head

If I notice how God designed the human body, I realize the head is physically situated above my heart. This is a good analogy for me to focus on in my life. Keeping my head above my heart helps me in certain situations. If I let my heart guide me, sometimes I get hurt. Today I will work at keeping my head above my heart.

My Intent For Today:

1.

_____

2.

_____

3.

_____

Evening - Teaming Up with God

God and I make an excellent team. God knows the best plans for me even when I do not. As God puts faith, trust and love in me, I put my faith, trust and love in God. Together we make a beautiful duo. The only other one who spends the most time with me, other than me, is God. Oh, how happy this makes me!

Today I Am Grateful For:

1.

_____

2.

_____

3.

_____

May 14th

Morning - Calm

Working on my serenity maintains my sanity. Today I try my best to work at keeping calm no matter how my day unfolds.

My Intent For Today:

1.

_____

2.

_____

3.

_____

Evening - Counting My Blessings

As I close my eyes and end my day, I reflect on the things that I have done during this day. I take a look to see if there are things I could have done better/differently. If there are, I do not begrudge myself. Instead I remind myself that tomorrow is a new day to change myself and how I do things. I reflect on the things I did today that I am proud of and honor my achievements. I remind myself to repeat those kinds of things again since they served me well. Tonight, I take into account my day, both the good and not so good. I count my blessings and remind myself how grateful I am for this day. In everything that happens, there is a blessing or a lesson.

Today I Am Grateful For:

1.

_____

2.

_____

3.

_____

May 15th

Morning - Fit
I work today to stay **FIT** ...

Fearless/Faithful   Faithful
Inspired   Intuitive
Thankful   Trusting

My Intent For Today:
1.

_____

2.

_____

3.

_____

Evening - Feeling My Emotions
I experience many different emotions and most times my emotions are SPOT ON. Allowing myself to experience my emotions and express the after effects of an emotion is what takes work. Often I can shut down my negative emotions very quickly so as to NOT FEEL THEM. The pain of negative emotions is sometimes unbearable. By shutting down, I may be doing myself a disservice. Instead, I may want to work at getting better at expressing all of my emotions in a healthier way. For example, if I am angry, I can release my anger elsewhere, like on the tennis court or by exercising. This allows me to release the negative emotion in a way that serves a dual purpose ... exercise is healthy for me. I will examine how I feel and express my emotions ... ALL OF THEM ... positive and negative.

Today I Am Grateful For:
1.

_____

2.

_____

3.

_____

May 16th

Morning - Searching for Answers

There are times when I ponder things, searching for answers. I realize that searching for answers is not time well spent because I do not need to have all the answers. Often when this happens, I get frustrated and that serves me no real purpose. Today I will make the most of the time I have. I will do my best to stay in the day and be the best version of me. I will try to keep the focus on myself in a healthy way so that if I am called upon to focus on others, the "best me" shows up. A tolerance for frustration helps me become a better me.

My Intent For Today:
1.

2.

3.

Evening - Run or Skip to God

When life is not good, run towards God for love, for assurance, for comfort. When life is good, skip towards God to share your love, your happiness, your comfort with God.

Today I Am Grateful For:
1.

2.

3.

May 17ᵗʰ

Morning - Grateful, Love and Pray

Today I will …
Be Grateful,
Be Happy,
Be Kind,
Make Positive Memories.
Show Love,
Breathe,
Smile.
Pray,
Reflect, and
Meditate.

My Intent For Today:

1.

2.

3.

Evening - Faith

Faith keeps me in touch with God. Faith is knowing that God is always with me.

Today I Am Grateful For:

1.

2.

3.

May 18ᵗʰ

<u>Morning - Bless</u>

BLESS my Neighbor …

Begin with prayer

Listen to them

Eat—share a meal to develop relationships

Serve—by listening I learn how to serve others

Share my story and share my love

BLESS can also mean …

Body—pray for health

Labor—pray for work

Emotional—pray for emotional health

Social—pray for my relationships

Spiritual—pray for spiritual health

My Intent For Today:

1.

_____

2.

_____

3.

_____

<u>Evening - Worrying is a Crime</u>

Worrying about things that have not yet happened robs me of enjoying living in the moment.

Worrying is like replying to a text that has not been delivered, or answering a phone call when the phone has not rung.

Today I Am Grateful For:

1.

_____

2.

_____

3.

_____

May 19ᵗʰ

Morning - Grief
Grief is like a roller coaster and sometimes it is rougher in the beginning. Grief has highs and lows, ups and downs; the lows may be deeper and longer. Grief is also like the waves of the ocean—sometimes the waves are small and rhythmic. At other times, the waves are strong and powerful—like tidal waves—which cause me to feel overwhelmed. I go through stages—denial, anger, bargaining, depression and acceptance. There are emotional and physical symptoms of grief. They can come on simultaneously or not.

EMOTIONAL SYMPTOMS OF GRIEF:

1) Shock and disbelief
2) Sadness
3) Guilt
4) Anger
5) Fear

PHYSICAL SYMPTOMS OF GRIEF:

1) Fatigue
2) Nausea
3) Lowered Immunity
4) Weight Loss/Gain
5) Aches and Pain
6) Insomnia

My Intent For Today:
1.

2.

3.

Evening - Behaviors
Breaking unhealthy behaviors is hard; creating healthy ones is even harder AND I am worth it.

Today I Am Grateful For:
1.

2.

3.

May 20ᵗʰ

Morning - Kindness

Today I will share my spiritual qualities with the world. I will share kindness and love with all those I meet.

My Intent For Today:

1.

_____

2.

_____

3.

_____

Evening - Giving Thanks

The way I can slow time down is by living, truly living, in the moment. I slow down my thinking, my physical movement, my breathing, and my heartbeat. I become calmer and less hurried. I am thankful for having more time. When I become more thankful, I become more "timeful." By giving thanks, I give myself the gift of full attention and this does slow down time for me. All my life experiences are God's gifts of time to me. I give thanks to God tonight for time.

Today I Am Grateful For:

1.

_____

2.

_____

3.

_____

May 21st

Morning - Feelings

I am learning to let my feelings show in a way that is healthy for me. I am realizing that being strong can mean I show my vulnerability and that it is okay to not always be in control. I am discovering that when I shed tears for whatever reason (grief; happiness; an emotional scene in a movie; a proud "parent"/"spouse" moment, etc.) the tears are an expression of a feeling that needs to be released and these tears are cleansing. I am seeing that by sitting with my feelings, I am allowing myself the opportunity to gain more experience in "feeling my feelings." By doing all these things, I am truly being human.

My Intent For Today:

1.

_____

2.

_____

3.

_____

Evening - Gratitude

I learn to keep my hands open and thankful in gratitude for ALL that comes my way. Thank you, God, for all my life's experiences, the good ones and the not so good ones. I give thanks to God for being there with me always.

Today I Am Grateful For:

1.

_____

2.

_____

3.

_____

May 22ⁿᵈ

Morning - I Choose

Today I choose to be happy.

Today I choose to be kind.

Today I choose to be a better person and version of me.

Today I choose to be kind and gentle with myself first.

Today I choose to maintain my serenity and peace even in the midst of strife and chaos.

Today I choose to share my serenity and peace with others I meet today along my travels.

Today I choose to love myself first and share my love with others.

Today I choose to try and do all of the above ... and be happy with simply trying.

Today I choose to do something.

Today I choose to do nothing.

Today I choose to simply be me.

My Intent For Today:

1.

_____

2.

_____

3.

_____

Evening - Happiness

True happiness comes from a feeling of gratitude. Being grateful creates a feeling of happiness. Tonight I am grateful. Tonight I am happy. Tonight I am joyful.

Today I Am Grateful For:

1.

_____

2.

_____

3.

_____

May 23rd

Morning - My Thoughts

My beliefs and thoughts are mine and mine alone. They are not for anyone to criticize, comment on, decipher, or even agree with. They are simply my thoughts. The only thing I need to focus on is knowing that the thoughts are mine and I can own them. Some of my thoughts are good and some not so good. They come and go like the waves of the ocean. My thoughts do not have to own me or my serenity. I am comforted knowing that my serenity is mine and is not dependent on my thoughts.

My Intent For Today:
1.

_____

2.

_____

3.

_____

Evening - Helping Others

Helping others is a good character trait. I am a human being and I like to help others. I am able to help in the best way I can. I need to set boundaries and know that I can only help those who accept my help. Helping someone who does not want my help is enabling and does not really work well. Tonight I will remember it is great to be helpful in the best way I can to those who ASK for my help. For others who I think may need my help, I can offer it, pray for them, and support them from afar.

Today I Am Grateful For:
1.

_____

2.

_____

3.

_____

May 24th

Morning - Being Truly Rich

The true riches in my life are NOT the things I can buy. My health (physical, emotional and spiritual) is what enriches me to be the best I can be. My faith enriches me with the trust that God's plan is working well. My love and compassion enriches me to grow in ways I never thought possible. Today I am thankful for being truly rich: rich in mind, body and spirit. This richness, that cannot be measured in monetary value, is priceless.

My Intent For Today:

1.

2.

3.

Evening - Peace and Happiness

The light of peace and happiness is always inside me burning bright. It is up to me to increase the flame when I feel the need. My peace and happiness are in my control, no one else's. I have the ability to maintain my peace and happiness because the pilot light is always on. I will remember this concept and use it as often as necessary. The more I feel inner peace and happiness, the more I can share with the world.

Today I Am Grateful For:

1.

2.

3.

May 25ᵗʰ

Morning - Blessing of Today
Instead of focusing on all the bad, be thankful for all the good. Each day is a blessing from God. It is a gift that slowly unfolds and reveals itself—one minute at a time.

My Intent For Today:
1.

_____

2.

_____

3.

_____

Evening - Hope, Healing and Helping
When I have **HOPE**:
Healing
Offered through
Positive
Energy

I am able to increase my inner peace and have the energy to bring others **HOPE**:
Helping
Other
People
Everyday/Everywhere

HOPE is a beautiful concept that flows from my inner peace. But I make sure I do not allow hope to cloud my judgment. I will exercise my **HOPE** in the way that serves me best. **HOPE** is a gift I give myself and in turn I can give to others.

Today I Am Grateful For:
1.

_____

2.

_____

3.

_____

*May 26*th

Morning - Bliss
BLISS means:
Believing
Love
Infuses
Simple
Serenity

My Intent For Today:

1.

2.

3.

Evening - My Heart ♡
When something touches my heart ♡, I welcome it.
When my heart is not into it, I say goodbye to it.
Let it come, let it come, let it come into my heart.
I say hello to happiness.
Let it go, let it go, let it go from my heart.
I say goodbye to my fears and sadness.
I love God. I love me. I love life with all my heart ♡.

Today I Am Grateful For:

1.

2.

3.

May 27th

Morning - Responsibility

As I mature in my spirituality, I realize that the only person I am truly responsible for is ... ME. Even if I am a daughter/son; wife/husband; mother/father; or sister/brother; I am still only responsible for myself. Yes as a parent, I have a responsibility for the care of my children, but it is limited to the point of my children becoming independent. Like a mother bird cares for her young until they are ready to fly and journey into the world on their own, so is my responsibility as a parent. My children will always be loved by me unconditionally and have been entrusted to me by God, but they are God's children first. God always has HIS/HER hand on each of HIS/HER children. Today I will remember that the one person I am truly responsible for is ME. I will entrust my loved ones into the care of GOD.

My Intent For Today:
1.

2.

3.

Evening - Forgive

I do not know what tomorrow will bring. I shall not stay mad for too long. I shall learn to forgive and love with all my heart. I will not worry about the people who do not like me. I will enjoy the ones who do love me.

Today I Am Grateful For:
1.

2.

3.

May 28th

Morning - Colors of the Rainbow

The colors of the rainbow that appear after a heavy rainfall have meaning. Red releases my fears. Orange helps me experience joy and releases shame and guilt. Yellow cleanses my emotional pain and increases my security. Green brings me balance, inspiration, and also renews my love and brings me forgiveness. Blue enhances my self-expression and allows me to speak my truth. Indigo encourages healing and self-awareness. Violet stimulates my wisdom and serenity. White releases my pain, heals my hurts, and offers peace to my spirit. Each color has a purpose. A rainbow is a spectrum of color that can bring happiness, wisdom, clarity and a spiritual connection to my life. I will look to the hope and strength of the rainbow next time I am in need of positive energy. I need not look far. I can always find a rainbow emoticon on my smartphone and there it is. Today I will take the colors of the rainbow with me throughout my day.

My Intent For Today:

1.

_____

2.

_____

3.

_____

Evening - Faith, Hope and God

Faith is a deeper sense of hope as in saying "I hope it works out" versus "I have faith it will work out." The latter has a much deeper and more sincere meaning.

Faith + Hope = GOD

Today I Am Grateful For:

1.

_____

2.

_____

3.

_____

May 29th

<u>Morning - Positivity</u>

Every human is beautiful in a unique way. It is helpful for me to recognize that every human goes through difficult times. I try to keep a positive outlook on my day even when I may be having a challenging one. Having positive energy helps me, especially when there may be people around me who are not positive. Today I will do my best to share my positivity with those I interact with. I will also do my best to not allow someone's negativity affect me.

My Intent For Today:

1.

_____

2.

_____

3.

_____

<u>Evening - Honesty</u>

The truth does not change, but how honest I am with myself does. Honesty is an ongoing process.

Today I Am Grateful For:

1.

_____

2.

_____

3.

_____

May 30th

Morning - Thankfulness

Waking up to the sounds of birds chirping, a plane flying overhead or a train passing through makes me grateful to be alive for one more day—a new day gifted to me from God that has been planned just for me. If something happens that makes me sad or angry, I can choose to sit in the emotion or feel it in a healthy way and move forward with the rest of my day. If something happy happens, I can feel the happiness in the healthiest way for me and share that feeling of happiness with anyone I meet today. This is the way I can share my positivity, allowing it to grow within me, and then share it with others. Today I will appreciate the gifts 🎁 I receive, including all of the emotions, and be **THANKFUL**.

My Intent For Today:

1.

_____

2.

_____

3.

_____

Evening - Happiness

My happiness lies in me comparing myself only to ME!
I am happiest when I compare myself to ME!

Today I Am Grateful For:

1.

_____

2.

_____

3.

_____

May 31ˢᵗ

Morning - Gentle with Me

Each new day is an opportunity for me to begin a new chapter in the book of my life's journey. When I realize that I am the author and that the only character I am responsible for developing is ME, I begin to embrace this concept more readily. If this book were to be made into a movie, the only person who could truly portray ME is ME. I am the best person who knows who I am, how I feel, and how I want to be. Today, I will use love and kindness to develop into the ME I want to be. I will be gentle with myself as this better version of ME continues to grow and develop.

My Intent For Today:

1.

2.

3.

Evening - Discovery

One's road in life leads to different paths. Some parts of the road are smooth and some bumpy. Some parts of the road are lonely and less traveled and other parts are subject to heavy traffic. One thing I know—I am never traveling in my discovery alone—God is always there guiding me to take the path that God knows is BEST for ME!

Today I Am Grateful For:

1.

2.

3.

JUNE

GRATITUDE

June 1st

Morning - Worry

Worry is like a wilting flower—it serves no purpose. Faith and hope are like blooming flowers—they bring belief.

My Intent For Today:

1.

_____

2.

_____

3.

_____

Evening - Self-Reflection

As the day comes to a close, I can take time to reflect on my day. What have I done today that I am proud of? Happy about? Wish I could change? Would I like to take back my actions? What did I not do today which could have made a difference as to how my day played out? Was I the best version of me that I could be? Did I try my best? What can I take from today that will help with my tomorrow? What can I leave in this day that will help me tomorrow? As I close the chapter on today, I take refuge in knowing that I have done this self-reflection with integrity and will not be too judgmental with myself. I know that the lessons I can learn from and the blessings of today are all good for my growth.

Today I Am Grateful For:

1.

_____

2.

_____

3.

_____

June 2nd

Morning - Letting Go of My Fears

When I let go of my fears, my inner peace begins to flow.
When I go with the flow, my serenity begins to show.
When my thoughts begin to race, I know it is time to go slow.
The more I can do this, the more I will grow.
If I find myself feeling low, I count my blessings, and my inner light and happiness begins to GLOW.

My Intent For Today:

1.

2.

3.

Evening - Crying Allows Me ...

The sound of a newborn baby's first cry is music to parents that their baby is healthy. Then after that first cry, parents try to comfort their children and soothe them when they are crying. WHY? Tears may not be a bad thing. Crying allows me to let the emotion flow from the inside out. I am not told to hide my happiness and laughter—so why am I encouraged to dry my eyes? The next time I see someone crying, it is okay to offer them a tissue. It may not be okay for me to tell them not to cry.

Today I Am Grateful For:

1.

2.

3.

June 3rd

Morning - DOG is GOD Backwards for a Reason

Dogs want to be close to us. They get excited to see us. They like to jump up when we are near. They like to please us.

Dogs try to understand us. Dogs are good listeners when we speak. They do not "talk" over us.

Dogs do NOT understand why we get upset at the things they do. When we scold them, they soon forget and show us love and come back to be near us again.

Dogs test our boundaries, like the way we do with God.

Dogs always miss us—no matter how long we have been away. This is the same way God always loves us and remembers us—no matter how long we have been away from God.

Dogs belong to us. We own them. They are ours. We belong to God. God created us.

Dogs come when we call them. Do we come when God calls us?

Dogs always find their way home. We too can always find our way back to God.

Dogs, like God, give us unconditional love.

Dogs, like God, protect us.

My Intent For Today:

1.

_____

2.

_____

3.

_____

Evening - Master Mathematician

Every human being can be a master mathematician. All they have to do is count their blessings.

Today I Am Grateful For:

1.

_____

2.

_____

3.

_____

June 4th

Morning - How Others Impact Me

It is amazing that people whom I have never seen with my eyes can have an impact on me, just by me reading or hearing their words. They can be friends of friends, or authors, or simply God's messengers. Today I may read something that impacts how I carry myself throughout my day.

My Intent For Today:

1.

_____

2.

_____

3.

_____

Evening - Positivity and Happiness

With each day comes 86,400 seconds. My goal for each day is to take at least 5% of that each day ~ 4,320 seconds which is a little less than 1.4 hours, to share my positivity and happiness with others—especially those whom I know may be open to receiving my positivity and happiness.

Today I Am Grateful For:

1.

_____

2.

_____

3.

_____

June 5th

Morning - My Very Being

I am a child of God. I am not perfect and never will be. I will make mistakes. I will fall. I will fail. I will get hurt both physically and emotionally. I will try my best. I will keep learning. I will keep growing. I will be grateful for all the wonderful things in my life which contribute to my very being and to the person I am continuing to become.

My Intent For Today:

1.

_____

2.

_____

3.

_____

Evening - I Am Student and Teacher to Myself

When I awake, I begin a new day and I am in control of how I will express myself throughout the day. By the day's end I may have experienced a multitude of emotions. I have an opportunity at the end of the day to hold myself accountable as to where my emotions were expressed appropriately and where there was room for improvement. I can actually be both student and teacher to myself. By doing this simple exercise I can see lessons as well as blessings in the day I experienced.

Today I Am Grateful For:

1.

_____

2.

_____

3.

_____

June 6th

Morning - Exercising My Choices

As each minute of the day begins, I have the choice of how I want to be in that minute. I can choose to be happy. I can choose to push through sadness. I can ask for God's help if I feel I need it because God is always available to me. Today I will practice exercising my choices.

My Intent For Today:

1.

_____

2.

_____

3.

_____

Evening - Availability to God

God is always available to me. Am I always available to God? Tonight, I will make myself available to God.

Today I Am Grateful For:

1.

_____

2.

_____

3.

_____

June 7th

Morning - God's "Present" 🎁

Some days are more challenging than others. Some days are happier than others. Some days are busier than others. Some days are more peaceful than others. Some days are more sunny or rainy than others. One thing that is always constant is God's presence. Even when I think God is absent, God is present 🎁. I have to work harder at maintaining the connection and feeling God's eternal presence. I remind myself: when I am weak, God is strong; when I am happy, God is happier; when I am challenged, God is there for me. When I am at peace, it is because of God's blessing of peace in my life.

My Intent For Today:

1.

_____

2.

_____

3.

_____

Evening - The Role People Play

In life, I will realize there is a role for everyone I meet. Some will test me. Some will use me. Some will love me. Some will teach me. But the ones who are truly important are the ones who bring out the best in me. They are the rare and amazing people who remind me why it is worth it.

Today I Am Grateful For:

1.

_____

2.

_____

3.

_____

June 8th

Morning - Today's Choices

I have choices about life's situations that happen on any given day. What to eat for breakfast? What to wear? What to say to someone who is in pain? What to do to keep my serenity during the day? I have choices. Today I will try my best to make the best choices for me that help me be the best ME.

My Intent For Today:

1.

2.

3.

Evening - Spreading Happiness and Serenity to Others

My serenity and peace can be shared with others if they are open to receiving it. The ripple effects of positivity and peace are infectious in a very beautiful way. Sometimes all it takes is a smile to start the ripple effect. I am much happier spreading happiness and serenity to others. This act of kindness further stimulates my inner happiness and keeps the negative thoughts and feelings away at least for today.

Today I Am Grateful For:

1.

2.

3.

June 9th

Morning - Take My Time

Today I will take my time and not rush through my day. I will practice more patience, less frustration, more compassion, and less sarcasm. I will be more loving, I will slow my thinking down. I will speak softly and slowly. I will communicate more effectively this way. Today I will pick my time to enjoy my day.

My Intent For Today:

1.
_____

2.
_____

3.
_____

Evening - Faith is Power

Faith is power. I love when faith kicks in for me. Faith brings me closer to God. My faith keeps me calm, serene and hopeful.

Today I Am Grateful For:

1.
_____

2.
_____

3.
_____

June 10th

Morning - Breakfast of Serenity

The best breakfast for me is a plateful of peace and a cupful of serenity.

My Intent For Today:

1.

2.

3.

Evening - Blessed, not Stressed

The more blessed I feel, the less stressed I will be. I will focus on the blessings and stop stressing.

Today I Am Grateful For:

1.

2.

3.

June 11th

Morning - Smiles are Infectious

Today I will try to be the ripple effect of happiness and hope in the world. I will smile at someone I meet on my journey and watch how I will get a smile back. Smiles are infectious.

My Intent For Today:

1.

_____

2.

_____

3.

_____

Evening - Less is More

Sometimes it is best for me to speak less and listen more, to open my heart and hug the one who needs me to. I am learning that less is really more.

Today I Am Grateful For:

1.

_____

2.

_____

3.

_____

June 12th

Morning - Health, Time and People

There are three things in my life that truly matter and are finite: health, time and people. My health can fail me. Time is not infinite. People in my life will not be there forever. This does not mean I become negative. It means I take full responsibility for my health (physically, emotionally, mentally and spiritually). I make the most of my time in the healthiest way possible. I treasure the time with people in my life who matter to me the most. I matter to me. God matters to me. I love the time we spend together. It is what keeps me healthy. I think this is why God has so many children. God knows there are those of us here for each other. God brings us together when God feels the time is right and we are healthy to receive.

My Intent For Today:

1.

2.

3.

Evening - Faith is …

Faith is not something that I can see. Faith is something I feel. Faith is not visible to me. Faith is in me. Faith has power. Faith connects me to God. Faith brings me closer to God. My faith tells me tomorrow will be a good day.

Today I Am Grateful For:

1.

2.

3.

June 13th

Morning - Doubt

When I found myself doubting things it is because my faith and hope are temporarily displaced. I remind myself that God does not doubt me, so why should I?

My Intent For Today:

1.

2.

3.

Evening - Ending My Day

As I get ready to end my day, it is nice to know that while I put my body to sleep, my mind sleeps as well. While I am sleeping, God is at work preparing a beautiful day for me for tomorrow.

Today I Am Grateful For:

1.

2.

3.

June 14th

Morning - Improving One's Health

Creativity is the best use of the imagination.
There are six things I can do to improve my overall health and to ensure staying healthy.

1) To get a good amount of sleep each night
2) To practice meditation or stress management
3) To practice yoga and focus on breathing
4) To practice emotional awareness
5) To eat healthy foods
6) To connect with Mother Nature

These six things can keep me healthy and can maintain my overall well-being.

My Intent For Today:

1.

_____

2.

_____

3.

_____

Evening - Healing Emotions

Healing emotions are joy, love, happiness and faith. Negative emotions, such as hurt, fear, anger or sadness can lead to inflammation and pain. Eating colorful foods is healthy for me. Connecting with Mother Nature leads to better health for me as well.

Today I Am Grateful For:

1.

_____

2.

_____

3.

_____

June 15th

Morning - Reality

Reality is an awareness of having an experience. Reality is having an awareness of going beyond thoughts. Awareness is the presence in which the mind, body and universe arise. Meditation puts me in touch with my soul. My body and mind are my experiences. Focusing on these four things: reality, awareness, meditation, body and mind can bring me overall well-being and health.

My Intent For Today:
1.

_____

2.

_____

3.

_____

Evening - Moments

On any given day, I have good moments and moments that are not so good. At the end of the day, the way I prepare for peaceful sleep is by changing my clothes, brushing my teeth, and saying my gratitude prayers. I also take my not so good moments, reflect, and then remove them from my mind. I focus on the positive and turn everything else off.

Today I Am Grateful For:
1.

_____

2.

_____

3.

_____

June 16th

Morning - Feelings and Moments

There are feelings and moments in life I remember. There are feelings and moments in life I try to forget. All the feelings and moments in my life carry a purpose; a lesson and/or a blessing. I have the choice of how these feelings and moments determine or affect the rest of my life.

The feelings and moments I try to forget have a deep impact and can actually make me stronger if I take time to explore them. My happier feelings and moments bring joy and serenity to my life. If I take the time to work and understand this, I will manage my life in a healthier way.

My Intent For Today:

1.

_____

2.

_____

3.

_____

Evening - Balance

My body is an experience and my overall well-being is best maintained when I keep a balance in my physical, emotional, mental and spiritual health.

Today I Am Grateful For:

1.

_____

2.

_____

3.

_____

June 17th

Morning - PUSH

The word **PUSH** means ...

Praying	**P**ray
Unconditionally	**U**ntil
Secures	**S**omething
Happiness	**H**appens

Today I will **PUSH** myself more to grow spiritually.

My Intent For Today:

1.

_____

2.

_____

3.

_____

Evening - It is All About the Words in the Dictionary

CALM is a four-letter word and comes before PANIC in the dictionary. PANIC is a five-letter word and leads to negative energy. TRY is a three-letter word and is a great thing to do. The word DO is a two-letter word. GOD is a beautiful three-letter word that sits between CALM and PANIC, and I is a fantastic one-letter word. Actually, let us add LOVE, a four-letter word. Both I and LOVE fall between GOD and PANIC. I, TRY and DO my best to stay CALM and let GOD LOVE ME when I may PANIC!

Today I Am Grateful For:

1.

_____

2.

_____

3.

_____

June 18th

Morning - Angel 😇 on Earth

I will start today and be an angel 😇 on earth. I will take the time to appreciate the goodness in someone else. I will let someone know they are loved. I will send someone I know a positive, endearing message. It will make them and me feel good.

My Intent For Today:

1.

_____

2.

_____

3.

_____

Evening - The Gifts 🎁 of My Life

I have received so many gifts 🎁 in life from the day I was born. The gift of breathing and the gift of air to breathe. This is a special gift which I may take for granted. I do not really focus on how or why I breathe. The awareness of breathing is truly enlightening. When I am calm, my breathing is slow. When I am physically active, my breathing is fast. When I am anxious/nervous, my breathing can be erratic. When I am happy/excited, my breathing is more rapid. It is essential to understand my own breathing and its rhythm to help me in times when I am feeling "something." I will try and focus on my breath; NOT take it for granted; and be grateful I am breathing. I will inhale what I need, and exhale what I no longer wish to keep.

Today I Am Grateful For:

1.

_____

2.

_____

3.

_____

June 19th

Morning - My Role on Earth 🌍
What is my role on Earth 🌍?
Why am I here on Earth?
How can I contribute to Earth?
Why do my contributions matter?
When will my contributions matter?

I ask myself these questions and it gives me choices on how I can improve and change myself for the better. My changes may have an impact/effect on those who travel on any part of life's journey—whether the part they travel on is for a minute, an hour, a month, years or my entire life. I want to make positive changes.

My Intent For Today:
1.

_____

2.

_____

3.

_____

Evening - I and Me
"I" and "Me" comes before "You" in the dictionary. I need to keep the focus on ME, before I focus on you, unless the You is God.

Today I Am Grateful For:
1.

_____

2.

_____

3.

_____

June 20th

Morning - Keep Track and Focus

If I keep track of all the good things I do for others and keep track of things that others are NOT doing for me, am I being judgmental? When I keep the focus on me and my actions and not think about the whys and hows of others' actions or lack of action, I will keep myself healthy. My ability to be kind, loving, compassionate, caring, etc. is truly something in my control and is not dependent on anything or anyone, except me. The best way others can catch on to what it is I like, is for me to do what I like. Leading by example of my actions is what works best. Today I will keep the focus on me and track **my actions**—NO ONE ELSE'S.

My Intent For Today:

1.

2.

3.

Evening - Spiritual Trip

When I want to move away from the dysfunctional world in which I can so easily find comfort, I take a trip and travel my spiritual path where serenity and calmness reside and I feel warm and welcome. The advantage of this trip is there are no long security lines and no need to pack a suitcase. I actually travel extremely light, leaving all the troubles behind. When I choose to return, I bring back with me life-long souvenirs—serenity, calmness and peace. These gifts 🎁 are priceless and I can always travel my spiritual path for more.

Today I Am Grateful For:

1.

2.

3.

June 21st

Morning - The Longest Day of the Year

June 21st is the longest day of the year. If I can make the most of today, I am capable of making the most of any day, no matter how much or how little daylight there is in the day. I realize there is more time in this day to spend with God and I will do my best to enjoy our relationship.

My Intent For Today:

1.

_____

2.

_____

3.

_____

Evening - True Potential

True potential comes from within and moves outwards to others and to the world.

It takes effort to make things simple. It is easy to make things hard. I will do my best to keep my true potential simple.

Today I Am Grateful For:

1.

_____

2.

_____

3.

_____

June 22ⁿᵈ

Morning - Holidays

Holidays can be fun.
Holidays can be difficult.
Holidays can be work.
Holidays can be painful.
Holidays can be peaceful.
Holidays can be stressful.

The actual day of the holiday is simply a 24-hour day. It is my holiday to be spent in a way that is healthy for me. Keeping it simple; not trying to make everything perfect for everyone; doing the best we all can; is all we can do best. Giving myself permission to take care of myself during the holiday is the real gift 🎁.

My Intent For Today:

1.

_____

2.

_____

3.

_____

Evening - Improving Myself

When I work on improving myself, I have no time to criticize or judge others.

Today I Am Grateful For:

1.

_____

2.

_____

3.

_____

June 23rd

Morning - Feel the Pain

When I try to avoid feeling hurt or angry, I can actually cause myself more harm. I postpone facing my pain. When I blame others for how I am feeling or try to punish others who may not have anything to do with how I am feeling, I may be doing this to maintain a sense of control. I do not have to let my emotional pain cripple or numb me. I find it helpful and healing to feel my pain. When I take responsibility for my feelings, I become emotionally stronger. When I allow myself time to sit in the discomfort of my feelings, figure out how to find a solution and move through it, I begin to heal from the pain.

My Intent For Today:

1.

_____

2.

_____

3.

_____

Evening - Peace and Positivity

Every moment is a new beginning. It is up to me to take the steps necessary to lead me in a good, positive direction. When I do this, it guides me to an inner peace that keeps me centered when LIFE's happenings unfold.

Today I Am Grateful For:

1.

_____

2.

_____

3.

_____

June 24th

Morning - Attainable Goals

It is healthy for me to have attainable goals. It is unhealthy to have goals that are beyond my reach or my capabilities. Unhealthy goals can lead to failure and disappointment. There are lessons to be learned from our failures. Today I will focus on healthy, attainable goals.

My Intent For Today:
1.

2.

3.

Evening - 24/7 it is Me!

I am the only person who actually spends 24/7 with me. Who else can truly judge me, other than me? The best way for me not to judge myself is to try and be the best version of me every day.

Today I Am Grateful For:
1.

2.

3.

June 25th

Morning - Feelings are Powerful

Feelings are powerful. Some feelings appear to be so real and strong that they can be alarming to me. Other feelings are fleeting. What I find helpful when I am in the midst of an uncomfortably strong feeling is to take a pause and a deep breath or two. I ask myself, "Why am I feeling this way?" "What possibly brought on the feeling?" and "How can I change how I am feeling or move past it?" Usually after asking these questions, either the feeling goes away or I am able to not react hastily. This obviously takes work and yet I am so worth it. Today I will take a pause ✿ when a feeling comes on that is not sitting well with me. Lastly, I will remember that some of my feelings are welcomed visitors and others are uninvited guests who must leave ASAP.

My Intent For Today:

1.

_____

2.

_____

3.

_____

Evening - God and Me

The difference between my plan and God's plan decreases as my connection/relationship with God increases.

Today I Am Grateful For:

1.

_____

2.

_____

3.

_____

June 26th

Morning - The Key 🔑 to Happiness

The key 🔑 to happiness is to close the doors to those in my life who tamper with the lock to my heart and try to rob me of my peace. I will safeguard my peace and unlock my heart to those with whom I feel comfortable.

My Intent For Today:

1.

_____

2.

_____

3.

_____

Evening - Focus

FOCUS means ...

Full	Faith	Finally
Ownership	Often	Overcoming
Cultivates	Cultivates	Chaos
Unique	Understanding	Using
Spirituality	Serenity	Serenity

Today I Am Grateful For:

1.

_____

2.

_____

3.

_____

June 27th

Morning - Pray

The simplest way to do something nice for someone is to pray for them, send positive energy and thoughts out to them, and have compassion for them.

When it comes to those who bring negativity to me; my best approach is ...

I stay away,
and I pray .
Stay away from them,
and pray for them.

My Intent For Today:

1.

_____

2.

_____

3.

_____

Evening - Peace

What is **PEACE**?

Practice	**P**ositive	**P**lease
Encouragement	**E**nergy	**E**xercise
And	**A**lways	**A**bsolute
Compassion	**C**reates	**C**are
Everywhere	**E**ncouragement	**E**veryday

Today I Am Grateful For:

1.

_____

2.

_____

3.

_____

June 28th

Morning - Healing Through Feeling

Once I have experienced something I cannot "un-experience" it. For example, once I have experienced peace, happiness, or love, I cannot "un-experience" it. Once I have felt pain, anger, or rejection, I know what it feels like and cannot "un-experience" it. When I get down on myself and become self-critical, I remind myself to reflect on one of my positive traits. When I focus too much on my assets and begin to become complacent or full of myself, I remind myself that I am a simple human being who is subject to making mistakes. I try my best to keep myself balanced so as not to lean one way or the other. My heart is meant to feel. My heart is also meant to heal. My heart can show love and can be broken. My mind can be open like my heart; my mind can also be closed which can lead me to pain or poor choices. Keeping both my mind and heart open allows me to be able to better handle my feelings. Being open shows my sensitivity which is an asset. Sensitive people are able to express themselves better and not close themselves off to their feelings. When I feel, I can heal. When I feel, I can be real.

My Intent For Today:
1.

2.

3.

Evening - Self-Care

Putting myself first does not mean I do not care. Putting myself first, means I DO CARE!

Today I Am Grateful For:
1.

2.

3.

June 29th

Morning - Spiritual Math

When things are not adding up, I start subtracting those things that I do not need. I focus on multiplying my joys, dividing my sorrows, and counting my blessings.

My Intent For Today:

1.

2.

3.

Evening - Gift

Every person that passes through my life makes a contribution to my life's stories. There are those who play large roles and make deep impressions; others may make a brief meaningful connection before life takes them in another direction. It is a rare gift when they suddenly reappear in my life after a long absence. They may never know what they bring into my life, but the renewed contact is a gift. I thank God for all the gifts in my life. God being the best one.

Today I Am Grateful For:

1.

2.

3.

June 30th

Morning - Faith

When I am afraid, I take my fears to God because God can handle them and I have faith in God.

I pray for my heart to be open; for my eyes to see the best in people; for my ears to listen carefully; for my hands to be helpful; for my mind to be pure; for my voice to be heard; and for my soul to always trust in God.

I am totally human. I make mistakes. I am not perfect. I cannot be perfect always because I deal with other human beings.

I am finding a happier balance. I am healthier. I am faithful.

My Intent For Today:

1.

_____

2.

_____

3.

_____

Evening - Love ♡ Myself

If I keep being everything to everyone, I forget about being something to the most important someone ... ME. Today I will do at least one nice thing for ME, even if it is a simple look into the mirror to say "I love you," or to give myself a loving hug.

Today I Am Grateful For:

1.

_____

2.

_____

3.

_____

JULY

FAITH

July 1st

Morning - Friendship

The best ways I have learned to help my friends are by lending an ear, giving a hug, or simply by being there. I thank all my friends who have been there for me. I love them all. Paying it forward is definitely the way to go.

My Intent For Today:

1.

2.

3.

Evening - Divine Appointments

Dear God,

I trust You. I love You. I have faith in You. Thank You for the many "Divine Appointments"(the people) You bring into my life. Thank You for the gift of free will/choice to decide if I want to keep, cancel, shorten or extend any of the "Divine Appointments" You offer me.
With love,
Your humble child

Today I Am Grateful For:

1.

2.

3.

July 2nd

Morning - This Moment

This moment, this minute, this hour, this day will NOT come again. I will enjoy the moments, minutes, hours and days as much as I can. I choose joy. I choose peace. I choose happiness. I choose serenity. I will be grateful I did.

My Intent For Today:

1.

_____

2.

_____

3.

_____

Evening - Keeping Watch

Watch my thoughts: they become words. Watch my words: they become actions. Watch my actions: they become habits. Watch my habits: they become character traits. Watch my character traits: they become my destiny. My destiny is part of God's plan.

Today I Am Grateful For:

1.

_____

2.

_____

3.

_____

July 3rd

Morning - Control

Control and the ability to relinquish control are two very different things. God has all the control. When I realize that God always has control, I am able to turn over my control.

My Intent For Today:

1.

_____

2.

_____

3.

_____

Evening - Prayer and Meditation

Through prayer, meditation and journaling, I tap into and deepen my spirituality. Sometimes I hear God's voice or see God's signs while I am in the shower, or while I am walking, or while I am working. I take time in my day to listen to or see the message. God's wisdom guides me to know what to do and when to do it or to simply do absolutely nothing.

Today I Am Grateful For:

1.

_____

2.

_____

3.

_____

July 4th

Morning - My Independence and Spiritual Freedom

Every day is Independence Day for me when I consider my spiritual freedom. I am free to think my own thoughts while creating and visualizing new ideas. I remain open to divine guidance, trust and follow my intuition. I thank God every day for the blessing of spiritual freedom. Today I do my very best to reach my own personal freedom.

My Intent For Today:

1.

_____

2.

_____

3.

_____

Evening - Give Joy, Laugh More and Share the Light

Healthy living happens when I give **JOY**, **LAUGH** more and share my **LIGHT** with others.

JOY:	LAUGH:	LIGHT:
Just	**L**ove	**L**aughter
Observe	**A**lways	**I**nspires
Yourself	**U**nleashes	**G**od's
	God's	**H**appy
	Happiness	**T**ruth

Today I Am Grateful For:

1.

_____

2.

_____

3.

_____

July 5th

Morning - Staying Healthy

A good way to stay healthy is to be good to myself by not pushing myself, by getting enough sleep, by eating good foods, by drinking plenty of water, by focusing on my serenity breaks from work, and by LOVING MYSELF.

My Intent For Today:

1.

_____

2.

_____

3.

_____

Evening - Dear Me, Fall Asleep

Dear Me,

Let me think of all the good moments I experienced on this beautiful day. Let me fall asleep with a smile. Let me awaken to a new tomorrow with that same smile.

Today I Am Grateful For:

1.

_____

2.

_____

3.

_____

July 6th

Morning - I Push Myself

Today I will do one thing that challenges me to be a better person. I do this so I can push myself to grow a little bit every day.

My Intent For Today:

1.

2.

3.

Evening - The Gift 🎁 of God

GOD is the 🎁 **GIFT** …

GOD	**G**race
Is	**I**nstills
Forever	**F**aithful
There	**T**rust

Today I Am Grateful For:

1.

2.

3.

July 7th

Morning - I Am a Little Crazy

Today I will try to be a little CRAZY.

CRAZY to me means ...

Courageous
Romantic
Awesome
Zealous
Young-at-heart/**Y**outhful

My Intent For Today:

1.

2.

3.

Evening - A Grateful Heart

Today, I began my day with a grateful heart, mind, body and soul.
Tonight, I will end this day with a grateful heart, mind, body and soul.

Today I Am Grateful For:

1.

2.

3.

July 8th

Morning - Simple Advice

The only time I give advice nowadays is if I am asked for it. If I do not live it, I do not give it. This is simple and works extremely well.

My Intent For Today:

1.

2.

3.

Evening - Serenity is Knowledge

Serenity is the knowledge of God's unconditional love for ME.

Today I Am Grateful For:

1.

2.

3.

July 9th

Morning - I Become Happier

I become happier by being more patient, by reducing my expectations, and by keeping myself healthy. I work at it. The payoff is the smile on my face.

My Intent For Today:

1.

_____

2.

_____

3.

_____

Evening - Who is in Control?

When I realize that God is in control, nothing can be out of control, especially ME.

Today I Am Grateful For:

1.

_____

2.

_____

3.

_____

July 10th

Morning - The Answer is Love ♡

No matter what the question, the answer can be **LOVE** ♡.

LOVE means to me …

Love   Learning
Offers   **O**thers
Valuable   **V**alue
Energy   **E**mpathy

My Intent For Today:

1.

_____

2.

_____

3.

_____

Evening - Good Morning, Good Night

When I wish someone a good morning, good afternoon or goodnight, I am really offering them what I want for myself first. I now look in the mirror in the morning as I brush my teeth, and at night before I go to sleep, and say "Good Morning" and "Goodnight" to ME. It truly makes me feel good, and allows me to put myself first at the beginning and end of the day.

Today I Am Grateful For:

1.

_____

2.

_____

3.

_____

July 11th

Morning - Time for Me
The time between when I wake up and actually get out of bed is time for ME. I make the most of this ME time by inviting myself into God's world to jumpstart our day together.

My Intent For Today:
1.

_____

2.

_____

3.

_____

Evening - What Makes Me Happy
When I do something for me that makes me happy, I am loving myself. The only person that can make me truly happy is ME. The only person who knows what makes me happy is ME. But with God's guidance, becoming happy is much simpler.

Today I Am Grateful For:
1.

_____

2.

_____

3.

_____

July 12th

Morning - Accepting Others

When I become more accepting of others, my judgment diminishes, and others seem to judge me less too.

My Intent For Today:

1.

2.

3.

Evening - The Time I Spend

The time I spend thinking about things that are bothersome deprives me of time I spend on things that bring me joy. These moments are lost. If I spend my moments in healthy ways, I am happy and at peace.

Today I Am Grateful For:

1.

2.

3.

July 13th

Morning - Worry, Who Me?

Worry is a waste of time and energy. Time can be better spent on being happy or doing things that make me happy. I let God do the worrying for me. God does a better job of worrying than I ever could.

My Intent For Today:

1.

2.

3.

Evening - What Negativity Can Develop ...

Good things can be developed from negative situations. An example of this is childbirth—it is painful yet the pleasure is the baby that is born. Compassion and forgiveness can develop from negative situations which may ultimately lead to personal freedom and peace.

Today I Am Grateful For:

1.

2.

3.

July 14th

Morning - The "Haves" and the "Wants"

If I keep dwelling on what I do not have, I cannot focus on obtaining what I want. More importantly, God always has what I need, even when I think I need nothing.

My Intent For Today:

1.

_____

2.

_____

3.

_____

Evening - Someone's Anger

When someone is angry and expresses misdirected anger at me, it is usually because they are unhappy with themselves. I am learning to walk away from the situation, instead of becoming a target for someone else's anger. I can offer my smile instead of engaging with the person. This can diffuse the person's anger. If it does not work, I can walk away and preserve my serenity.

Today I Am Grateful For:

1.

_____

2.

_____

3.

_____

July 15th

Morning - My Default Setting

Today is the day made just for ME. I can reset my default settings to work better for ME. This reset feature is in my control. It is in my hands. It is up to me. Today, I will restore/reset my default settings as needed. I will keep my day as simple as only I can. My serenity is my default setting today. I will work at staying in this default setting.

My Intent For Today:

1.

2.

3.

Evening - Time with Myself

If I really want to know who I am or who I want to be, I spend time with myself. Time spent alone is the time I have to discover who I really am. I am not trying to prove anything to anyone, nor am I trying to impress anyone. When I am with myself, I am free to be my true self. If I do not like who I am, I am free to change this and no one is with me to judge the changes I am making.

Today I Am Grateful For:

1.

2.

3.

July 16th

Morning - Being Comfortable

When I am not comfortable with the choices I make, I create doubt. When doubt is created, fear can creep in. When fear comes into the picture, the decisions I make may not be the smartest ones for me. Fear brings discomfort. This is when it is best to take a pause. This is when I can reflect on the choices available to me. Being uncomfortable with the choices I make and keeping faith in my choices will lead me on the right path. When I have faith, I have comfort. When I have comfort, I make better choices.

My Intent For Today:
1.

_____

2.

_____

3.

_____

Evening - Accepting and Expecting

I am getting better at accepting the unexpected. I am improving my ability to accept more and expect less.

Today I Am Grateful For:
1.

_____

2.

_____

3.

_____

July 17th

Morning - It is All About Me

If I do not believe in myself, how can I expect others to? If I do not trust in myself, how can others trust me? If I do not love me, how can others love me? Today, I will believe, trust, and love ME. God does and so can I.

My Intent For Today:

1.

_____

2.

_____

3.

_____

Evening - Decision Making

Tonight If I am not feeling at my best physically, emotionally or spiritually, I will not make any important changes or long-term decisions. It is always better for me to feel at my best when making important decisions or changes. Even when I make a decision, I can take some time before I carry out the decision. This gives me some time to reflect on my decision before I act on it. There is a big difference and time between making a decision and carrying it out. This time is "patient reflection."

Today I Am Grateful For:

1.

_____

2.

_____

3.

_____

July 18th

Morning - My Patience and My Attitude

I am realizing that I become a better version of me when both my patience and attitude improve. When I am grateful for the things I have, the people in my life, and the plan that God has for me, I am able to be more tolerant of the situations, circumstances and people that test my patience. Today, I will improve my level of patience and my attitude of gratitude. I will watch how working on these two attributes will make me the person I am meant to be.

My Intent For Today:

1.

_____

2.

_____

3.

_____

Evening - Serenity Through Acceptance

When I become more accepting of things I cannot change, I become more patient. The more patient I become, the more peace I obtain. The more peace I have, the better I become at focusing on myself and the things I can change. The more I change the things I can, the stronger I become. The stronger I am, the more serenity I can maintain. Serenity is achieved through acceptance.

Today I Am Grateful For:

1.

_____

2.

_____

3.

_____

July 19th

Morning - The Absence of ...

Courage is the absence of fear. Light is the absence of darkness. Hope is the absence of helplessness. Compassion is the absence of anger. Love is the absence of hate. Faith is the absence of doubt. Today I will practice having more courage, hope, compassion, love and faith. I will let God light the path for me.

My Intent For Today:

1.
_____

2.
_____

3.
_____

Evening - Increased Faith Leads to Deeper Patience

When I accept people for who they are and see things/situations as they are, I become more composed in my choices. I have an increased faith in myself. This increased faith and acceptance are the biggest factors that lead me to a deeper level of patience.

Today I Am Grateful For:

1.
_____

2.
_____

3.
_____

July 20th

Morning - Unsettling Situations

When a situation unsettles me and part of it is out of my control, it is important for me to do something else. By doing something else, I am practicing patience, until the situation resolves.

My Intent For Today:

1.

2.

3.

Evening - The Day Ends

When the day ends, I reflect on what I have done well and what did not go well. I forgive myself for things I would have done differently. I applaud myself for the good deeds I practiced with self-compassion, self-love and self-care. I also go to sleep knowing that the new day dawns with a clean slate and is a fresh start for me.

Today I Am Grateful For:

1.

2.

3.

July 21st

Morning - Being Better
Today I will work on being better than I was yesterday. Tomorrow I will work on being better than I am today. This way I am always growing.

My Intent For Today:
1.

2.

3.

Evening - Positivity
Before I go to sleep, I will end my night with a positive thought. This way, the last thought I have before the evening ends is a positive one. I like ending the day the way I started the day, POSITIVELY.

Today I Am Grateful For:
1.

2.

3.

July 22nd

Morning - Hope

Keeping HOPE alive makes the new day brighter even on a cloudy morning. A good way to stay hopeful is to be faithful and this is beautiful.

My Intent For Today:

1.

_____

2.

_____

3.

_____

Evening - Three Things to Keep Me Healthy

These three things keep me physically, emotionally and spiritually healthy:

1) Learning from my actions of yesterday
2) Living for the day today
3) Looking for a better tomorrow

Today I Am Grateful For:

1.

_____

2.

_____

3.

_____

July 23ʳᵈ

Morning - Someday is Today

I often feel that today could be the SOMEDAY I have been waiting for. I sometimes feel today is my tomorrow and the chance to do things better than I did yesterday.

My Intent For Today:

1.

_____

2.

_____

3.

_____

Evening - When I Am

If I can smile when I am crying, if I can laugh when I am hurting, if I can hug my loved one when I am angry, I will become a better person by focusing on releasing the negative and becoming more positive.

Today I Am Grateful For:

1.

_____

2.

_____

3.

_____

July 24th

Morning - Improving My Life Through Change

The way my life improves is by me changing for the better. Today, I will focus on making a small positive change in my life purely for me.

My Intent For Today:

1.

_____

2.

_____

3.

_____

Evening - The Reasons to Change

Tonight I realize these are reasons to make a change in my life:
I have learned from my past
I have been hurt enough
I need to stop the insanity
I need to move forward and be the change

Today I Am Grateful For:

1.

_____

2.

_____

3.

_____

July 25th

Morning - An Emotional Breath

When I let go, I am able to breathe better emotionally. When I keep holding on, I deprive myself of emotional oxygen. The more I let go, the deeper an emotional breath I can take which leads me to inner peace and serenity.

My Intent For Today:

1.

_____

2.

_____

3.

_____

Evening - My Maturity

Tonight I can reflect back on my past and truly understand why certain things happened the way they did. I call this enlightened growth or maturity. My maturity helps me smile through my tears, laugh through the chaos, and believe that the things occurring today are for good reason. I may understand this better by tomorrow.

Today I Am Grateful For:

1.

_____

2.

_____

3.

_____

July 26th

Morning - My Struggles

My struggles strengthen me physically, emotionally and spiritually. My struggles allow me to look inwards and upwards instead of feeling down and out. My struggles can lead me to a path of peace, freedom and serenity.

My Intent For Today:

1.

_____

2.

_____

3.

_____

Evening - Have Faith, Have Love

There are times in my life when I have been afraid, have loved, and have lost. Tonight I will do my best to have faith, to have love, and to find something that helps me grow.

Today I Am Grateful For:

1.

_____

2.

_____

3.

_____

July 27th

Morning - Kindness and Compassion

There is kindness. There is compassion. Compassion is kindness with a touch of LOVE. Today I will try to be compassionate, not just kind. By practicing compassion, I bring myself more serenity.

My Intent For Today:

1.

2.

3.

Evening - Making Choices and Mistakes

I will make choices that make the most sense for me. I may make mistakes. I will not berate myself for the choices I make. There are always lessons and blessings in the choices I make. I am doing the best, my best, and that is all I can do.

Today I Am Grateful For:

1.

2.

3.

July 28th

Morning - Uplift and Inspire

Most people rarely give thought to the effect their actions have on others. When I am friendly, helpful and responsive, I effortlessly create an atmosphere around myself that is both uplifting and inspiring. When I take a few moments to contemplate how my individual behaviors affect the people I spend time with each day, I come one step closer to seeing myself through the eyes of others. Something as simple as my smile can affect someone else's day.

My Intent For Today:

1.

_____

2.

_____

3.

_____

Evening - Love and Life

Love is like life. It is not always easy. It does not always bring happiness, but if I do not stop living, why should I stop loving?

Today I Am Grateful For:

1.

_____

2.

_____

3.

_____

July 29th

Morning - More Peace and Serenity

On this day, I realize the more love I give out, the more love comes back to me when I need it most. The more sharing I do, the more others share with me when I need it most. The more accepting I am of others, the more accepting others are of me when it is most needed. The more peace and serenity I show, the more peace and serenity I have when I need it most. Today I realize these things. I am maturing with each day.

My Intent For Today:

1.

_____

2.

_____

3.

_____

Evening - Full Deep Breaths

Tonight I take the time to take full deep breaths. I breathe in peace and serenity. I breathe out the negative thoughts. I count my blessings as I breathe and I sleep in peace.

Today I Am Grateful For:

1.

_____

2.

_____

3.

_____

July 30th

Morning - Today My Prayer is

Today my prayer is "God help me do the next right thing." It is not what I say that counts, it is what I do. The quality of my life can be affected by what I do in the next ten minutes. Thus, I only look ten minutes ahead.

My Intent For Today:

1.

_____

2.

_____

3.

_____

Evening - Stay Present

The best gift 🎁 I am giving myself tonight is ... to stay PRESENT.

Today I Am Grateful For:

1.

_____

2.

_____

3.

_____

July 31st

Morning - Today is a Gift 🎁

Today is a gift 🎁 to open and discover. I will let this day unfold and I will BE PRESENT. I will slow down to truly enjoy the moments as they unfold. If I get stuck during this day, I will close my eyes, take a pause, and then open my eyes and discover that the rest of the day is another gift 🎁 for me to open and enjoy.

My Intent For Today:

1.

2.

3.

Evening - I Am Myself

If I practice loving myself, then others can love me when I am myself.

Today I Am Grateful For:

1.

2.

3.

AUGUST

PEACE

*August 1*st

Morning - Joy

Joy is a beautiful gift I can experience in many different ways. Joy feeds my heart. Joy may be quiet, like a child sleeping peacefully. It may be boisterous, like shared laughter that brings tears to my eyes. Joy is an experience of my heart and soul. Joy is an experience of God's presence. Joy is always a thought away. When I am experiencing stress, I can pause and remember the joyful moments in my life. When I think of the kindnesses given and received, joy lifts my spirits and brings me even more JOY.

My Intent For Today:

1.

2.

3.

Evening - Useless or Use Less

When I look at the word USELESS, and break it down, it becomes USE LESS. I would rather USE LESS words, energy and actions that do NOT serve me well, else I may become USELESS. When I USE LESS, I maintain my personal USEFULNESS.

Today I Am Grateful For:

1.

2.

3.

August 2ⁿᵈ

Morning - Share My Best

Today I will do my best to share my smile, my hugs, my laughter, my joy and my time with all those whom I encounter along my path.

My Intent For Today:

1.

_____

2.

_____

3.

_____

Evening - Creating a Circle of Love

Through giving, I receive. I share the blessings I have received and create a circle of love and giving that can expand outwards. This circle of love helps to bless me and everyone in my world.

Today I Am Grateful For:

1.

_____

2.

_____

3.

_____

August 3ʳᵈ

Morning - Wear My Spirituality Cloak

I will wear my spirituality like a CLOAK, because God's love for me is no JOKE. I feel warm with God's spirit upon me.

My Intent For Today:

1.

_____

2.

_____

3.

_____

Evening - Being Kind

Tonight I rejoice in being kind. I will be kind to myself. I will be kind to others. I will do my best to be the best I can be. I will "BE" through my actions. My actions say a lot about me. Others' actions say a lot about them. I will focus on being ME.

Today I Am Grateful For:

1.

_____

2.

_____

3.

_____

August 4th

Morning - Maintaining Serenity, Compassion, and Gratitude

Today I practice maintaining my serenity, compassion and gratitude. This takes my focus off of anything that may be giving me discomfort or concern. My serenity softens me. My compassion calms me. My gratitude guides me to a better place and space.

My Intent For Today:

1.

2.

3.

Evening - Completing the Day

As my day comes to a close, I take solace in knowing that I tried my best given the events of the day and the people I interacted with. Today may not have unfolded the way I intended or had planned for and yet I completed the day and I am able to reflect on it. As I fall asleep, I know that I am in God's care and I know that God has a good plan for my day tomorrow.

Today I Am Grateful For:

1.

2.

3.

August 5ᵗʰ

Morning - Grief Surfaces

Grief can surface at any time and at any place. It can actually surface because of a song I hear, a place I used to go, a person I met that knew my loved ones, or when a bird or butterfly appears. Anything can make my grief surface. This can simply be my mind and heart being gently reminded of all the LOVE I shared and the imprint this person left upon my heart. My grief can actually be seen in this positive light and thus I allow myself to feel the memories and the love that I still have in my heart always. I also know my loved ones are in a better place and are simply watching over me from up above.

My Intent For Today:

1.

_____

2.

_____

3.

_____

Evening - A Peaceful Night of Sleep

Tonight before I go to bed, I take a few moments to reflect on the day. I also take a few minutes to ask myself what I hope for the day tomorrow. I then ask God's help for tomorrow and focus on a peaceful night of sleep.

Today I Am Grateful For:

1.

_____

2.

_____

3.

_____

August 6th

Morning - My Inner Compass

I can seek the answers to life's questions by looking outside of myself and seeking advice from others. As a unique individual, with my own personal stories, my own sense of right and wrong, and my own way of experiencing life, looking to others for answers is only partially helpful. The answers to my personal questions can be most often found by looking within myself. I have an inner compass that I need to look to instead of searching outside of myself. If I can learn to listen, trust, and embrace the wisdom that lives inside me, I will be able to confidently navigate my life. *I will look in and up, not down and out.*

My Intent For Today:

1.

_____

2.

_____

3.

_____

Evening - Acceptance

When I learn to truly accept myself for who I am, two things can happen:

Others can accept me as well, AND

Through my acceptance, I can learn to change things about myself that serve me no purpose.

Today I Am Grateful For:

1.

_____

2.

_____

3.

_____

August 7ᵗʰ

Morning - My Bells 🔔 and Whistles

When I am feeling concerned, worried or afraid about something, I take the time to feel the fear, but not for too long because fear is not factual. Fear is an emotion that can be crippling to my spirit. I turn up my spirituality dial when my fear kicks in and this usually weakens my fear. Like a car has different bells and whistles to let us know the car is working well or needs attention, so do I have my own bells 🔔 and whistles that I need to attend to when I hear/feel them go off. It is prudent to pay close attention to them and take care to address them.

My Intent For Today:

1.

_____

2.

_____

3.

_____

Evening - All in a Day's Work

At the close of the work day, I take pride in knowing that I made it through the day's work. I may not have completed all the tasks, but as long as I tried my best, then it was a good day of work. The new day ahead gives me another opportunity to work at a healthy pace. Tonight I will rest easy knowing work keeps my mind focused on good things that deserve my attention. For now, I will sleep and let God work.

Today I Am Grateful For:

1.

_____

2.

_____

3.

_____

August 8th

Morning - Unhealthy Territory

Sometimes I experience concern, anxiety, and even fear while waiting for a medical test result or undergoing a test. My concerns generally arise about unknown results, yet I am allowing my mind and emotions to go into unhealthy territory. Instead I recall happy memories or I look to things that I am grateful for presently in my life. This helps keep me calm and rest my mind from the issue at hand. I apply this concept to other areas of my life and it allows me to maintain calmness and serenity.

Sometimes my heartache or pain leads me to renewed faith which leads me to deeper serenity. God, lead me to the path that will keep me faithful. If I lose my way and stray from You, help me to use my God Powered Strength (GPS) to find my way back to You, God.

My Intent For Today:

1.

_____

2.

_____

3.

_____

Evening - Stop , Drop and Roll

When I stop ⬤ the anger, drop the fear, and roll away from the anxiety, I am able to achieve my goal ... SERENITY.

Today I Am Grateful For:

1.

_____

2.

_____

3.

_____

August 9ᵗʰ

Morning - Today
Today I can enjoy my life. Today I can handle challenges that come my way. Today I can help strangers, family, friends, by putting myself first. Today I am able to show more compassion to others. Today I can walk away from those who are toxic to me. Today I can do all of these things thanks to my strong spirit, right mental attitude, and overall good physical well-being.

My Intent For Today:
1.

_____

2.

_____

3.

_____

Evening - Options and Choices
Options and choices are two different things. Options can be explored before making a choice. I may make a choice based on the options available to me. I no longer feel the need to rush the choices I make. I have less regret about the choices I make because I take the time to do what is best for me.

Today I Am Grateful For:
1.

_____

2.

_____

3.

_____

August 10th

Morning - Life Unfolds

My life unfolds every single day like the way a dog stretches SLOWLY
as he/she awakens. If I allow each day in my life to unfold SLOWLY,
I am likely to enjoy life more and face my challenges better as well.
Today I will encourage myself to UNFOLD the day SLOWLY and
therefore ENJOY it more. The words UNFOLD, SLOWLY and
ENJOY are calming to me.

My Intent For Today:

1.

_____

2.

_____

3.

_____

Evening - Less Control, More Peace

When I relinquish my control, my inner peace grows. I sometimes
have to lose something (control) to gain something else (peace).
Basically, the less I control, the more at peace I am.

Today I Am Grateful For:

1.

_____

2.

_____

3.

_____

August 11ᵗʰ

Morning - Passing Judgment

When others pass judgment on me, I realize it is not really judgment. It is possibly envy. Perhaps they want something I have—peace, serenity, gratitude, love, and compassion. I work hard for the "something" and those who are judging me do not realize the hard work that goes into obtaining and maintaining these amazing traits. So I will show compassion towards them. And if I cannot, I can ask God to take care of being compassionate towards them. This usually works well for me.

My Intent For Today:

1.

_____

2.

_____

3.

_____

Evening - Path to Serenity

The best way to maintain a healthy body is by exercising properly. The best way to have a peaceful mind is by cultivating good mental habits. These good mental habits lead to a path of serenity.

Today I Am Grateful For:

1.

_____

2.

_____

3.

_____

August 12ᵗʰ

Morning - Sharing Peace

Acceptance leads to serenity. Today I practice accepting others for who they are and what they are capable of doing. I learn each day that when I accept and truly understand what I can and cannot change, I have more serenity and peace. I am able to share that peace with others.

My Intent For Today:

1.

_____

2.

_____

3.

_____

Evening - Redirecting My Mind

Whenever my mind wanders towards wrong or negative thinking, I ⬢ STOP what I am doing. I can shift my mind, like I shift a car, into the wrong lane. To bring my mind back to clear thinking I put on my re-directional signal. This is not always easy. It takes self-discipline and much practice. I redirect my mind by taking a breath or two of fresh air, listening to an uplifting song, reading an inspirational book or saying the Serenity Prayer.

Today I Am Grateful For:

1.

_____

2.

_____

3.

_____

August 13th

Morning - Maintaining Peace and Serenity

Today I will work on maintaining my inner peace and serenity the same way I work to spread my peace and serenity to others. The way to do this is by:

Being consistently kind to others
Being helpful to others
Being appreciative of the efforts of others

I will try this today and let my inner peace grow.

My Intent For Today:

1.

2.

3.

Evening - Limiting Contact

I will spend my time with the right kind of people. If I cannot avoid some people, I can limit my contact/time spent with them. People who thrive in chaos, can destroy another person's serenity. I maintain my serenity by limiting my time with those who live with drama and chaos.

Today I Am Grateful For:

1.

2.

3.

August 14th

Morning - Change

God, grace those who harm me with blessings. God, please change me.

God help me do what I can and not torture myself about what I cannot.

My Intent For Today:

1.

___

2.

___

3.

___

Evening - Use My Time Wisely

Time is measured in hours, minutes and seconds. It is up to me to decide how I want to spend the hours, minutes and seconds. When I focus on negative things or exhibit negative emotions, I lose time keeping my serenity and gratitude. I will do my best to use my time wisely and maintain my serenity, gratitude and faith in the healthiest way possible. I will focus on staying healthy physically, emotionally and spiritually.

Today I Am Grateful For:

1.

___

2.

___

3.

___

August 15th

Morning - Living My Life

When I realize there are people and things in my life that I can lose, I learn to live my life more fully and I discover my true self. Living my life involves accepting how my life unfolds—ONE DAY AT A TIME.

My Intent For Today:

1.

2.

3.

Evening - Stir Up Peace and Serenity

When things happen that I do not feel comfortable with, I try to physically move away. I quietly pray, "God, tell me what to say or do, or guide me to say or do nothing." Simply doing this exercise helps me gently stir up my inner peace. It moves serenity up to the forefront of my mind.

Today I Am Grateful For:

1.

2.

3.

August 16th

Morning - The Supreme Force

My goal is to keep moving forward and to keep the Supreme Force close to me always as I walk through each day. This Supreme Force protects me, loves me, guides me, and keeps me safe always.

Thank You, God, for keeping me safe through the day and for creating a new tomorrow for me.

My Intent For Today:

1.

_____

2.

_____

3.

_____

Evening - Tonight, I Let God

Tonight I let God steer me away from any negative thinking and give me a peaceful sleep. I let God take over the work while I sleep. I can resume the work tomorrow.

Today I Am Grateful For:

1.

_____

2.

_____

3.

_____

August 17th

Morning - Love, Positivity and Confidence

Today I will use my inner strength and love to forgive myself and others who have harmed me. Instead of stirring a pot of negativity which can come to a boil, I will use positivity to bring joy to my life and help me through my day. Today I will walk, talk and carry myself with confidence. I can do this because I love and accept me for who and where I am in my journey.

My Intent For Today:

1.

_____

2.

_____

3.

_____

Evening - The Power of Ocean Waves

The rhythmic tempo and crashing of ocean waves carry goodness towards me and take back anything that is not healthy for me. These ocean waves can also be God's love flowing to me and then from me to others.

Today I Am Grateful For:

1.

_____

2.

_____

3.

_____

August 18th

Morning - I Am Responsible for Me

I am learning more and more that I am only responsible for my own feelings, behaviors and reactions—not anyone else's. This knowledge is very liberating, as well as a relief.

My Intent For Today:

1.

_____

2.

_____

3.

_____

Evening - God's Way

I am working hard each day to understand that all happens in God's time, not mine. I also realize that my way and God's way can be different. God's way is usually better for me.

I take serenity breaks during my day to help me "breathe." I often take a pause during a hectic day—it is like an "energy bar" for my mind and soul.

Today I Am Grateful For:

1.

_____

2.

_____

3.

_____

August 19th

Morning - My Five Senses

My prayer for today is to see the best in me and others with my eyes; to be a good listener with my ears; to speak kindly with my mouth and tongue; to express love and give hugs using my arms; to show compassion and forgiveness using my heart; to be open to learning using my mind; and to always have faith in God using my soul. I can pray this prayer starting now.

My Intent For Today:

1.

_____

2.

_____

3.

_____

Evening - A Happier Me

I become a happier me when I learn to accept what is, let go of the things I cannot change, and have faith and trust in the things that are to be.

When I increase my "Tolerance for Frustrations" dial on my mind, I am able to stay calm in the midst of chaotic situations. Controlling the dial is in my hand.

Today I Am Grateful For:

1.

_____

2.

_____

3.

_____

August 20th

Morning - Keep Myself Warm

When the weather is cold, even frigid, I do my best to stay warm. I take care of myself to make sure I do not feel the effects of the cold. I try to apply this when I am in a situation with someone who is cold towards me. I need to do my best to keep myself warm and not feel the effect of the coldness of others.

The best way for me to really love and live my life is to remove or stay away from negativity and evil. Yes that is why EVIL spelled backwards is LIVE.

My Intent For Today:

1.

2.

3.

Evening - God's Guidance

God, please guide me throughout my day, all day.
God, please guide me throughout my night, all night.
God, Your guidance is what makes my journey faith filled.

Today I Am Grateful For:

1.

2.

3.

August 21st

Morning - Being Prepared

When preparing for a snow storm, I make sure there is ample food in my home to feed my family, enough salt to de-ice my driveway, a clear path for me to walk, a full tank of fuel in my car, and marshmallows for sipping hot chocolate while I watch the snow fall. In other words, I prepare myself for the snow by taking proper care. I need to do the same in all areas of my life. Sometimes all I need to do to be prepared is to stay calm.

My Intent For Today:

1.

_____

2.

_____

3.

_____

Evening - Stillness of Peace and Letting Go

As night falls upon this day, there is a stillness that it brings. As I focus on the stillness, I become calm and have peace as I drift off to sleep. If I awaken from my sleep, I work on falling back to sleep with the same feeling of peace.

When I train myself to let go of everything I fear to lose, I become stronger and am able to handle loss when it happens to me.

Today I Am Grateful For:

1.

_____

2.

_____

3.

_____

August 22ⁿᵈ

Morning - God Keeps Me Safe

Remaining calm in pressured situations takes practice. If I take the time to sit down and feel my feelings, turn them into more positive emotions, and take deep breaths, I find myself becoming calmer. Fear can become anticipations, worry can become concern, and dread can become caution. I become calmer when my emotions become healthier.

My Intent For Today:

1.

2.

3.

Evening - Good Health

Good health is not all about diet and exercise. Good health can also be maintained by being grateful, maintaining calmness, protecting serenity, staying positive and focusing on inner peace.

Today I Am Grateful For:

1.

2.

3.

August 23rd

Morning - Five Easy Ways To Wellness

Five easy ways to my overall wellness:
1) Being in touch with nature
2) Interacting with positive people
3) Giving time to those in need
4) Staying active physically, mentally, emotionally, and spiritually through exercise, prayer and meditation
5) Learning new things to keep the mind active

My Intent For Today:
1.

2.

3.

Evening - Allowance

The same way I allow myself to be loved, I allow myself to be hurt. The choice is realizing how much love or hurt I need to stay healthy and grateful.

Today I Am Grateful For:
1.

2.

3.

August 24ᵗʰ

Morning - True Success

True success is measured by the experiences I have, the strength I gain, the gratitude I express, the love I share, and the inner peace and serenity I maintain. Today, I ask for God's help to protect me from myself and my doubts. Make me right in Your way, God, not mine. Amen.

My Intent For Today:
1.
_____
2.
_____
3.
_____

Evening - Exact Change

Change happens from the inside out, so I will initiate the change by starting with me. The next time I am asked "Do you have exact change?" I will say "Yes, I do. I am the change."

Today I Am Grateful For:
1.
_____
2.
_____
3.
_____

August 25th

Morning - The Journey

As my serenity deepens, my fear weakens. I realize my spirit is more reachable and, with God's assistance, more teachable. As my faith grows, my love for God shows. I am enjoying the journey of discovery and look forward to experiencing this new ME.

My Intent For Today:

1.

_____

2.

_____

3.

_____

Evening - Be the Light

I want to be the person who touches the lives and hearts of people. I want to be a positive light to others and put a smile on their faces. For in the end it is not what I say that matters. It is how my actions make them feel that will lovingly stay in their memory.

Today I Am Grateful For:

1.

_____

2.

_____

3.

_____

August 26th

Morning - Commit to the Changes

True transformation happens when I connect to the changes that I like and know will make me a better version of me.

If I always receive everything I want in my life, there will be no need for faith. Faith is being humble and knowing that there is something bigger than me.

How amazing would it be if I could take a "true selfie" of my inner beauty for myself to see? I will be able to transform myself so that the outside really is a reflection of my inside.

My Intent For Today:

1.

_____

2.

_____

3.

_____

Evening - Lamp of Light

Tonight I want to be a **LAMP** of **LIGHT**.

Love	**L**ove
Allows	**I**s
Me	**G**od's
Peace	**H**ealing
	Truth

Today I Am Grateful For:

1.

_____

2.

_____

3.

_____

August 27th

Morning - God Wake Me Up

God, wake me up with an open heart, clear mind and a willingness to learn.

May my Supreme Power fill me up with faith.

God, gently rock me to sleep tonight.

Today I ask God to feed my soul with faith and guide me throughout my day.

When I am at a loss for words, I pray to God to bring the words to me.

My Intent For Today:

1.

_____

2.

_____

3.

_____

Evening - Simple Ways To Pray

One of the simplest ways for me to pray is to speak my truth, even if the person I speak to is my own reflection in the mirror. At least one person is listening. Another simple way for me to pray is to write my prayers down and place them into a God box. I am leaving them to God to do what God feels is best for me. My prayers are always activated by my faith. My prayers are placed in the best hands ... God's Hands!

Today I Am Grateful For:

1.

_____

2.

_____

3.

_____

August 28th

Morning - Forgiveness

One simple way to bring about transformation in me is through forgiveness. Forgiveness brings me peace. It makes me more compassionate and empathetic. Forgiveness also helps me to be a healthy person instead of a person who is hurting.

I am most tranquil and at peace when my heart is open, my mind is flexible, and my body is firmly grounded upon the earth.

Peace and serenity fill me when my thoughts and actions are positively aligned and are in perfect harmony.

My Intent For Today:

1.

_____

2.

_____

3.

_____

Evening - Comfort and Confident

When I am comfortable with knowing who I am, I feel both confident and empowered. This strengthens me to tackle any challenges that come my way and to enjoy my life more fully and faithfully.

Today I Am Grateful For:

1.

_____

2.

_____

3.

_____

August 29th

Morning - The Passcode to My Happiness

With fears comes unrest and stress.

With serenity comes love, joy and peace.

When I close my eyes, I hear better, my sense of smell is stronger, my ability to meditate is deepened and I am able to feel the happiness of my mind.

The only person who knows the passcode to my happiness and serenity is me. No one else has access to my serenity without my consent.

My Intent For Today:

1.

_____

2.

_____

3.

_____

Evening - The Power of Self

Tonight I will take the time to know myself better, to define my core values as I know them to be, to value myself, to communicate effectively, to listen to myself, to honor myself, and to enjoy myself. By doing all of these, I become truly "**power-full**." This power comes to me in the healthiest way. The use of this power for myself is more refreshing, energizing and fun. This power is infused in me by my Higher Power.

Today I Am Grateful For:

1.

_____

2.

_____

3.

_____

August 30th

Morning - Things to Help Me Grow
Today I will try to do both of these things and grow.
1) To free my mind of people and situations that I cannot control
2) To extend my mind by learning something new that I always wanted to learn

My Intent For Today:
1.

2.

3.

Evening - Experience Happiness
As today comes to a close, I feel both blessed and grateful. I thank God for all the happenings of my day, even the things I may not have enjoyed or understood. Reflecting on my day, I can see the blessings and the lessons.
Tonight I will focus on love, happiness and joy as I fall asleep. I will reflect on the positive interactions of this day.

Today I Am Grateful For:
1.

2.

3.

August 31ˢᵗ

Morning - With God by My Side

Today, with God by my side, there is nothing that will happen that I cannot manage. I know God loves me unconditionally. Everything will be alright. I feel God's protection, guidance and safety. All is well. Positive affirmations said out loud in the morning in the mirror after I am dressed help me start my day properly. Some examples of positive affirmations are: I am healthy, I am filled with energy, I love myself, I am serene, I am happy.

My Intent For Today:

1.

_____

2.

_____

3.

_____

Evening - Love ♡ and Smiles ☺

I do my best to share my smile and love with others because in doing so love ♡ and smiles ☺ will come to me as well.

With a smile, I am reminded of the love I feel for myself. Tonight, I accept how this day has been and I look forward to a new day coming tomorrow.

Today I Am Grateful For:

1.

_____

2.

_____

3.

_____

SEPTEMBER

PATIENCE

September 1st

Morning - Regret

When I experience regret, I take some time to reflect, accept and take action to move in a positive direction. If I stay too long in the moment, I am not hearing the message and cannot move forward. Regret is about my choices. Regret happens when I do something that goes against my basic values and causes me unrest. Today I accept I will experience some regret and I will no longer fret.

My Intent For Today:

1.

_____

2.

_____

3.

_____

Evening - Prayers Help

Sometimes if I cannot ask for help, I ask for prayers instead. It helps to pray and prayers help. Both ways work. Prayers are helpful. Help is prayer.

Today I Am Grateful For:

1.

_____

2.

_____

3.

_____

September 2ⁿᵈ

Morning - Being Kind

I can truly be kind by thinking kindly, acting with kindness, and speaking with kindness. It all starts with ME being kind to ME.

My Intent For Today:

1.

2.

3.

Evening - My Emotional Needs

When I am absolutely at peace and happy, my emotional needs are being met.

The only one responsible for my emotional needs being met is me.

My life is constantly changing. My emotions are my built-in GPS that help me navigate through the ups and downs of life. I become emotionally stressed or weak when I fight the changes of my life.

Today I Am Grateful For:

1.

2.

3.

September 3rd

Morning - Kindness and Love

Today I will live my life more fully by experiencing and processing all my emotions. I will practice self-compassion by treating myself the way I would a loved one—with kindness and love.

My Intent For Today:

1.

2.

3.

Evening - Accepting My Emotions

When I accept that my emotions are inevitably an indicator of change, I build up my emotional stamina. The changes can be happy or sad and the corresponding emotions are, too. For example, a new job makes me happy while the loss of a job can be devastating.

Today I Am Grateful For:

1.

2.

3.

September 4th

Morning - Becoming Stronger

I become physically stronger when I lift weights. I become emotionally stronger when I lighten my emotional baggage. I become spiritually stronger, when I let God share my journey.

My Intent For Today:

1.

_____

2.

_____

3.

_____

Evening - My Many "Selves"

When I focus on myself, I put emphasis on:
   1) My physical self
   2) My emotional self
   3) My spiritual self
   4) My mental self

These four "selves," when nurtured by me, enable me to enjoy and appreciate my life.

Today I Am Grateful For:

1.

_____

2.

_____

3.

_____

September 5th

Morning - Remembering Loved Ones

I thank God for the memory of all my loved ones who are no longer physically present. I honor their memory and presence in my life by speaking their names when I miss them.

My Intent For Today:

1.

_____

2.

_____

3.

_____

Evening - All About Grief

Grief is a journey. The counterpart of grief is love. The depth of one's grief correlates to the depth of the love. The best way for me to go through my grief is to grieve. Grief does not always make me sad. It brings to my mind beautiful and happy memories of a loved one gone. These memories bring a smile to my face, tears to my eyes, and warmth to my soul.

Today I Am Grateful For:

1.

_____

2.

_____

3.

_____

September 6th

Morning - Breathe

A simple act of taking a breath is me moving forward. BREATHE! I breathe in what I am craving from God. I breathe out what I want to let go of and put into God's Hands.

My Intent For Today:

1.

2.

3.

Evening - Earth's Angels 😇

There are angels 😇 on earth. They are the people in my life who listen to my story. They believe in me. They love me without judging me. They see the goodness in me. Most of all, they travel some of their life's journey along with me. I may not even know some of these angels. The unknown angels are special because of the random acts of kindness they do for me.

Today I Am Grateful For:

1.

2.

3.

September 7th

Morning - Tired
When my body or mind is tired, I rely on my heart and spirit to lead me on my life's journey.

My Intent For Today:
1.

_____

2.

_____

3.

_____

Evening - As Night Falls
As night falls and my day's work is over, I take some time to sit with myself, be grateful and appreciate the work I accomplished today. Feeling gratitude is essential for my well-being. Tonight, I take time to thank myself for simply being.

Today I Am Grateful For:
1.

_____

2.

_____

3.

_____

September 8th

Morning - As Day Begins

As dawn breaks and my day begins, I take time to awaken the spirit within me. I am grateful for the restful sleep I had and I look forward to the day ahead. I thank God for today's possibilities.

My Intent For Today:

1.

2.

3.

Evening - Being Grateful

When I begin to feel overwhelmed, I take some deep breaths and remember moments of joy. This brings me comfort and serenity to handle my life better. Being grateful helps me make better choices.

Today I Am Grateful For:

1.

2.

3.

September 9th

Morning - Doing What is Best

Sometimes I have to do what is best for me and my life, not what is best for everyone else.

My Intent For Today:

1.

_____

2.

_____

3.

_____

Evening - The Spirit Within Me

The simple reason I am inspired is because of the spirit within me. The gift of inspiration sent as a spirit within me creates positive energy and allows me to bring hope to everyone in my life.

Today I Am Grateful For:

1.

_____

2.

_____

3.

_____

September 10th

<u>Morning - Good Morning, I Love You!</u>
When I look in the mirror this morning, I smile and say to myself, "Good morning, I love you!." The person in the mirror smiles back at me. It is a great way to start a beautiful day.

My Intent For Today:
1.

_____

2.

_____

3.

_____

<u>Evening - Prayers are Fast</u>
The fastest thing on earth is prayer because it reaches God even before we speak the words.

Today I Am Grateful For:
1.

_____

2.

_____

3.

_____

September 11ᵗʰ

Morning - A Day of Remembrance

On this day of remembrance, I take the time to remember all my loved ones gone. One of the ways I honor them and let their spirit live on is to incorporate their best character traits into my being. I add my own flare, of course. Their legacy lives on through me. If I want my legacy to be a positive one, I live positively starting today.

My Intent For Today:

1.

_____

2.

_____

3.

_____

Evening - Winding Down

Tonight, as I wind down, I am grateful for the ability to wind down.

Today I Am Grateful For:

1.

_____

2.

_____

3.

_____

September 12th

Morning - True Freedom
Complete honesty brings true freedom in any relationship.

My Intent For Today:
1.

_____

2.

_____

3.

_____

Evening - Remembering God
God always has a plan, a reason, a way of letting me know that God loves me. Remembering God is a great way of returning that love.

Today I Am Grateful For:
1.

_____

2.

_____

3.

_____

September 13th

Morning - My Happiness

My happiness keeps me healthy. Today I will work on my mental, emotional and spiritual happiness. I will also work on improving my physical health.

My Intent For Today:

1.

_____

2.

_____

3.

_____

Evening - Working for Myself

I can say I am self-employed. I can say I am my own boss and my own best employee. I am working on myself, for myself, and by myself, with God as my personal assistant always by my side.

Today I Am Grateful For:

1.

_____

2.

_____

3.

_____

September 14th

Morning - The Recipe for Life

The recipe for a beautiful life full of peace, love and serenity is:

1 Kg of Kindness	1 Heaping TBSP of Happiness
1 Jar of Joy	2 Gallons of Gratitude
3 TBSPS of Trust	4 Pinches of Positivity
1 Large Bowl of Blessings	1 Carton of Character
2 Pints of Patience	3 Cups of Love
10 Fingers Full of Faith	1 Cup of Understanding
½ Cup of Acceptance	⅓ Cup of Forgiveness
3 Small Bowls of Smiles	2 ½ Cups of Laughter

Mix ALL the above ingredients together and let the journey begin.

My Intent For Today:

1.

_____

2.

_____

3.

_____

Evening - A Simple Meditation

A simple meditation … a long drive with great music, an open mind and a pure heart.

Today I Am Grateful For:

1.

_____

2.

_____

3.

_____

September 15th

Morning - The Time to Change is Now
The best **TIME** to bring about change in my life is **NOW**:

TIME means:	**NOW** means:	
Trust	**N**ew	**N**eeds
In	**O**pportunities	**O**ver
My	**W**orking	**W**ants
Energy		

My Intent For Today:
1.

_____

2.

_____

3.

_____

Evening - Inhale, Exhale
When I inhale serenity and exhale worry, I am able to grow through whatever it is I am going through.

Today I Am Grateful For:
1.

_____

2.

_____

3.

_____

September 16th

Morning - The ABC's of Life

ABC's of a beautiful life:

Acceptance
Brings
Change

My Intent For Today:

1.

_____

2.

_____

3.

_____

Evening - Who Can Help Change Me?

If I am looking for one person who can help me change myself for the better, I simply stand in front of the mirror. I smile and I love the person smiling back at me.

Today I Am Grateful For:

1.

_____

2.

_____

3.

_____

September 17th

Morning - The Four C's of life:

Creating
Choices
Causing
Changes

My Intent For Today:

1.

_____

2.

_____

3.

_____

Evening - Seeking God

Too often I spend my time seeking God for an answer to my problem. All I should be doing is simply seeking God.

Today I Am Grateful For:

1.

_____

2.

_____

3.

_____

September 18th

Morning - Keeping My Distance

There is a good reason why it is wise to keep a safe driving distance from the car in front of me—to avoid an accident or dangerous situation. The same distance applies to negative people in my life ... keeping a safe distance helps.

My Intent For Today:

1.

2.

3.

Evening - Power and Peace

God's power over me brings God's peace to me!

Today I Am Grateful For:

1.

2.

3.

September 19ᵗʰ

Morning - It Begins and Ends with Gratitude

I begin my day with gratitude. I end my day with gratitude. What happens in the middle of the day is up to me.

My Intent For Today:

1.

_____

2.

_____

3.

_____

Evening - The Knapsack of Life

I will try to throw out things that I do not need from my knapsack of life. That makes my mind, body and soul feel lighter.

Today I Am Grateful For:

1.

_____

2.

_____

3.

_____

September 20th

Morning - God Will Show Me

Today I will tell God everything. I will hide nothing from God. God will show me all that I need to see and believe today.

My Intent For Today:

1.

_____

2.

_____

3.

_____

Evening - Be Silent and Listen

In the silence, my listening skills improve so I can hear God speak to me. In silence, my sight sharpens to see the signs God sends me. When I am silent, I can listen more attentively.

Today I Am Grateful For:

1.

_____

2.

_____

3.

_____

September 21ˢᵗ

Morning - Today I will be:

More grateful	More sensible
Less shameful	Less mournful
More thankful	More helpful
Less painful	Less tearful
More spiritual	More playful
Less doubtful	Less of a handful
More humble	More thoughtful
Less resentful	Less powerful
More careful	More grateful
Less intolerable	Less boastful

Finally, after practicing all of these, I will become more ... beautiful.

My Intent For Today:

1.

2.

3.

Evening - God Takes Away

God takes my anger, pain, shame and fear and sends me joy, love, trust, faith and hope.

Today I Am Grateful For:

1.

2.

3.

September 22nd

Morning - Seven Days A Week
Each day of the week has unique characteristics that make it a day God made just for me.
Simple Sunday
Magical Monday
Terrific Tuesday
Wonderful Wednesday
Therapeutic Thursday
Fabulous Friday
Serene Saturday

If my week goes like this, I know I have taken the time for me.

My Intent For Today:
1.

_____

2.

_____

3.

_____

Evening - Past, Present and Future
I will try to not let my past fill up my present, only to destroy my future.

Today I Am Grateful For:
1.

_____

2.

_____

3.

_____

September 23rd

Morning - Trust and Faith

I have TRUST and FAITH in God's presence in my life. With God's presence, I will make it through any situation. TRUST and FAITH lead me to HOPE.

My Intent For Today:

1.

_____

2.

_____

3.

_____

Evening - Faith and Grace

In deeper reflection, I notice that it is in my weakest moments with the grace of God I have been able to strengthen my faith. With my simple beliefs and strong faith, with my patience and grace, anything I strive to achieve is worth the chase!

Today I Am Grateful For:

1.

_____

2.

_____

3.

_____

September 24th

Morning - My Secret Magic Tricks

There are some secrets in life that are helpful. There are some tricks that I can use to make my life better. There is magic that I can perform to improve my life without being a magician. The secret magic trick is to practice more gratitude and acceptance of what I have today in my life. When I am stuck I practice gratitude and acceptance. If I am feeling sad, I practice gratitude and acceptance. If I am feeling gloomy, I try to practice gratitude and acceptance. If I feel like I am spinning my wheels, I try gratitude and acceptance. When I find myself getting frustrated, angry or resentful, I use the secret magic trick of gratitude and acceptance. Magically the feeling of frustrations, anger and resentment fade away. When my life seems complicated, I go back to the basics and simply practice gratitude and acceptance. Gratitude and acceptance are truly secret magic tricks that keep my life simpler and allow me to enjoy the journey.

My Intent For Today:

1.

_____

2.

_____

3.

_____

Evening - Take the Chance

I will trust my feelings, take the chance, love my life, and experience God's trance.

Today I Am Grateful For:

1.

_____

2.

_____

3.

_____

September 25ᵗʰ

Morning - Blessing My Past

Events from my past may linger, creating emotional barriers that prevent me from fully letting go and moving on. It is up to me to bless my past as a learning experience. It is my choice to let go of the pain from the past. I am ready, willing, and able to make courageous and mindful choices and move forward with peace of mind and positive intention.

Blessing my past, staying in the present, and looking forward to the future may work well for me.

My Intent For Today:

1.

_____

2.

_____

3.

_____

Evening - Prayer is the Key

Prayer is the key to unlocking the door to my connection with God. Focusing on God ignites the divine spark within me that illuminates the way to my serenity.

Today I Am Grateful For:

1.

_____

2.

_____

3.

_____

September 26th

Morning - Alignment of My Thoughts and Actions

Positive thoughts lead to positive words which lead to positive actions. It is important to periodically check the alignment of my thoughts, words and actions. If the alignment is proper, the positive energy can go viral. If they are out of alignment, I can always make an adjustment.

My Intent For Today:

1.

_____

2.

_____

3.

_____

Evening - Acceptance Brings ...

I am learning to appreciate the gifts acceptance can bring. Acceptance brings change. Acceptance brings understanding. Acceptance sparks communication. Acceptance sparks positive action. Acceptance sparks growth. Acceptance brings peace. Acceptance brings love. Acceptance brings serenity.

Today I Am Grateful For:

1.

_____

2.

_____

3.

_____

September 27ᵗʰ

Morning - Wake Up and Never Give Up

I have experienced things I never wanted to. I have gone through situations I never imagined I would have to. I have at some point felt all alone. I have dealt with people who simply did not treat me right. I have enjoyed many happy memorable moments too. Through it all I have experienced the ability to wake up, get up, dress up, show up, listen up, shut up (when necessary), grow up, and most importantly, look up (to GOD) and never give up.

My Intent For Today:

1.

_____

2.

_____

3.

_____

Evening - Thank God Tonight

I thank God every evening for keeping me safe through the night and for the gift of a new day tomorrow.

Today I Am Grateful For:

1.

_____

2.

_____

3.

_____

September 28ᵗʰ

Morning - Thank God Today

I thank God every morning for awakening me to see this beautiful new day and for keeping me safe.

My Intent For Today:

1.

_____

2.

_____

3.

_____

Evening - One's True Self

It always amazes me how a person's true self comes through when playing sports. Those who are aggressive in their life, show their aggression. Others who truly have serenity, enjoy playing and are not solely looking to win. These people are playing to have fun and stay healthy. Winning is a bonus. I will try my best to let my true inner self be the strong player on my team. I know that God is part of my amazing team. I know I am a part of God's team. Together we can make it.

Today I Am Grateful For:

1.

_____

2.

_____

3.

_____

*September 29*th

Morning - I Will Believe in Myself

Today, I will believe in myself. This is the best way for me to develop a healthy habit of changing myself and growing close to be the person God intends me to be.

My Intent For Today:

1.

_____

2.

_____

3.

_____

Evening - Tennis 🎾 is Like Life

The game of tennis 🎾 is like life. The terms used are: fault, service, advantage, let, great point, and love. In tennis, better players do their best to disguise their weaknesses and use their strengths. A player's endurance, serenity and patience show during intense long rallies. A good player knows what is needed to complete a great match. It is not all about winning. It is about enjoying the match played.

Today I Am Grateful For:

1.

_____

2.

_____

3.

_____

September 30th

Morning - Bitter or Better

My experiences can make me better or bitter. The choice is up to me.
I simply choose to be BETTER.

My Intent For Today:

1.

2.

3.

Evening - Guidance

Guidance = God U and I DANCE. There is a deeper **GUIDANCE**
that leads me to new discoveries of myself. This *guidance* fills me with
strength and serenity. If I am uncertain about a decision, I turn to
prayer. I turn within and then towards God. I realize that I am always
guided by the Divine Spirit available to me at any given moment.

Today I Am Grateful For:

1.

2.

3.

OCTOBER

SERENITY

October 1ˢᵗ

Morning - A Lovely Day Unfolds

I wake up today with the goal of having a lovely day. I will smile at a stranger. I will say thank you. I will do things slowly. I will give a compliment. I will laugh. I will be nice. I will be kind. I will listen well. I will wish someone a lovely day.

My Intent For Today:

1.

_____

2.

_____

3.

_____

Evening - God Always ...

I realize more and more that God never fails me. God is never late. God never leaves me alone. God never judges me. God always loves me. God always forgives me. God always believes in me.

Today I Am Grateful For:

1.

_____

2.

_____

3.

_____

October 2ⁿᵈ

Morning - I Can Have Peace

I can have peace even in spaces and places whether there is noise, chaos, or problems. Peace keeps my heart calm and mind clear to make sound choices, especially in difficult situations.

My Intent For Today:

1.

_____

2.

_____

3.

_____

Evening - Happy Things

Tonight I will recall three things that made me happy. I will reflect on my day. I will reflect on three things that I am proud of today. Doing this will bring me peace and serenity for a good night's sleep later tonight.

Today I Am Grateful For:

1.

_____

2.

_____

3.

_____

October 3rd

Morning - Saying Thank You

Today I will not only appreciate those who have shaped my life but also I will thank them for doing so. For me this includes saying a special thank you to God for not only being in my life, but for giving me life.

My Intent For Today:

1.

2.

3.

Evening - God Is In Control

I rest peacefully tonight remembering fully that God is in control. God is working on my behalf. God is preparing a beautiful new day for me to love, enjoy, appreciate and live. God's job is to work for me. My job is to wait patiently and remember God's work happens in God's time.

Today I Am Grateful For:

1.

2.

3.

October 4ᵗʰ

Morning - Today is for Me

Today is the oldest I have ever been and the youngest I will ever be again. Today I will be happy, laugh, love, smile and live my life fully. I will not get this day back. I want to be my best and make the most of this day. The entire day may not be happy or fun, but I can enjoy the parts of the day that are joyful.

My Intent For Today:

1.

2.

3.

Evening - Dear Mind,

Dear Mind,

The day has come to a close. I need to sleep peacefully. Please stop thinking now that night has fallen. Get some sleep and let God do the rest. Tomorrow is another day for us to begin working together again.

With love,

Your Spirit and Body

Today I Am Grateful For:

1.

2.

3.

October 5th

Morning - Move Past the Past

When I keep living in the past, I lose out on living in today. When I keep regretting the past, I do not learn from it. The best solution is to move past my past.

My Intent For Today:

1.

_____

2.

_____

3.

_____

Evening - Patience is ...

Patience allows me to handle the things that make me uncomfortable or endure the things that may cause me pain. Patience allows me to grow in ways I never knew I could. Patience is kindness to one's self. Patience is the presence of self-love and absence of self-deprecation.

Today I Am Grateful For:

1.

_____

2.

_____

3.

_____

October 6th

Morning - Good Morning God
Good morning, dear God,
Thank You for the blessings You bestow upon me today. I may not understand or appreciate them as they happen. I thank You in advance. Each blessing I receive, I humbly give You credit for. Amen.

My Intent For Today:
1.

_____

2.

_____

3.

_____

Evening - A Good Night
The best way I can truly have a good night is to relax my soul. I think of God lying beside me and I can have a peaceful sleep.

Today I Am Grateful For:
1.

_____

2.

_____

3.

_____

October 7th

Morning - Love or Obligation

Doing something for someone out of love rather than out of obligation always leaves me feeling better about myself. It makes me happy and I am grateful knowing this. I remind myself that people do not take advantage of my kindness unless I let them. I remind myself that people cannot mistreat me unless I let them. I remind myself that people cannot change me unless I let them.

My Intent For Today:

1.

_____

2.

_____

3.

_____

Evening - I Cannot Sleep

When my mind is overloaded I cannot sleep. When I am able to sleep peacefully my mind is in a deep state and I am connected to God.

Today I Am Grateful For:

1.

_____

2.

_____

3.

_____

October 8th

Morning - A Reason To

Every day I try to think of a reason to smile, a reason to laugh, a reason to love, a reason to be happy, a reason to be grateful, a reason to be joyful, a reason to be peaceful, and a reason to be hopeful. Doing this simple exercise gives me many reasons to stay positive.

My Intent For Today:

1.

_____

2.

_____

3.

_____

Evening - Changing Myself for Happiness

Just like I can change a light bulb when it burns out to restore light to a darkened room, I can change myself when I find my happiness needs to be restored.

Today I Am Grateful For:

1.

_____

2.

_____

3.

_____

October 9th

Morning - Faith

I believe that things happen for a reason. My trust in this, without needing to know why, is what I call FAITH.

My Intent For Today:

1.

_____

2.

_____

3.

_____

Evening - A Beautiful Life

I have a beautiful life because my life is beautiful!

Today I Am Grateful For:

1.

_____

2.

_____

3.

_____

October 10th

Morning - The Right Time
Waiting for the right time? The right time is when I stop focusing on waiting and start doing instead.

My Intent For Today:
1.

_____

2.

_____

3.

_____

Evening - Letting Go
Letting go of the painful memories of my past is like pouring sour milk down the drain. It brings me relief and makes room for gratitude and love.

Today I Am Grateful For:
1.

_____

2.

_____

3.

_____

October 11th

Morning - Having Control
I may have very little control over what happens in my life, but I do have control over how I feel or act in response to a situation.

My Intent For Today:
1.

_____

2.

_____

3.

_____

Evening - Blessings
Counting my blessings is always good. Sharing my blessings is better. Thanking God for my blessings is the best. When I share more, I have more.

Today I Am Grateful For:
1.

_____

2.

_____

3.

_____

October 12ᵗʰ

Morning - My Wants and Needs

My wants often exceed my needs. When I feel my prayers are not being answered, it is because God always gives me what God knows I need, not necessarily what I want.

My Intent For Today:

1.

_____

2.

_____

3.

_____

Evening - My Life Matters

Everything about my life matters and is important because I matter and I am important. I learn to ask myself what it is I need. I can make it a goal to move forward by taking the proper steps.

Today I Am Grateful For:

1.

_____

2.

_____

3.

_____

October 13ᵗʰ

Morning - Standing Up for Myself

I stand up for others sometimes better than I do for myself. I am learning that I need to stand up for myself. It keeps me emotionally healthier. I am the only one who knows my limits. Today I will stand up for myself with kindness, gentleness and confidence.

My Intent For Today:

1.

_____

2.

_____

3.

_____

Evening - Uncomfortable Situations

When I am in situations that are uncomfortable, reaching out for help is essential. When my first response is to ask for help, it makes all the difference. My vulnerability can lead to my serenity.

Today I Am Grateful For:

1.

_____

2.

_____

3.

_____

October 14th

Morning - PITY versus LOVE

PITY means …	**LOVE** means …
Pushing	**L**etting
Insecure	**O**thers
Thoughts	**V**oluntarily
Your way	**E**volve

Putting pity in the closet, lets the love flow.

My Intent For Today:

1.

_____

2.

_____

3.

_____

Evening - Keep It Simple

Tonight, I will keep it simple.
I will tell someone I love them.
I will call someone I have not spoken to in a while.
I will communicate more effectively to be clearly understood.
I will ask for help if I need it.
I will verbalize if something is bothering me.
I will enjoy my life and keep it simple.

Today I Am Grateful For:

1.

_____

2.

_____

3.

_____

October 15ᵗʰ

Morning - My Spiritual Homework

Some of the best spiritual assignments are:
Practicing forgiveness
Releasing anger
Being grateful
Speaking with God
Loving myself
Blessing those who have hurt me
Maintaining serenity during difficult situations
Practicing compassion
Listening to God
Turning my will over to God

My Intent For Today:

1.

_____

2.

_____

3.

_____

Evening - I Trust God

I trust God to guide me through all my life's situations, the happy and not so happy ones.

Today I Am Grateful For:

1.

_____

2.

_____

3.

_____

October 16ᵗʰ

Morning - The Past and Forgiveness

When I hold on to the past, I am unable to stay in the present. When I keep holding on to a grudge, I keep the wound open and the negative feelings cause me more pain. My heart stays closed and my mind hurts with the painful memory. Forgiveness is a spiritual tool that gives me freedom and an inner peace which leads to a happier me. Forgiveness releases the negativity and brings serenity to my life. It also brings me gratitude.

My Intent For Today:

1.

_____

2.

_____

3.

_____

Evening - Broken ♡ Heart

When something touches my heart, I welcome it. When something breaks my heart, I ask myself, "Was it worth it?" A broken heart ♡ can be mended with time. My broken heart ♡ can heal and there are lessons to be learned.

Today I Am Grateful For:

1.

_____

2.

_____

3.

_____

October 17th

Morning - Listening to My Body

When I am tired and not feeling well, I try and take it easy. Wearing myself down by doing too much never works well. I am learning to listen to my body. The body has much to say on any given day.

My Intent For Today:

1.

_____

2.

_____

3.

_____

Evening - Letting Troubles Go

After I let go of something that troubles me, I pray to God about it. I leave the situation alone. I trust God will take care of it in a way that is best for me.

Today I Am Grateful For:

1.

_____

2.

_____

3.

_____

October 18th

Morning - Experiencing My Life
It is a choice to have my life experiences make me bitter or better. I choose to be better at experiencing my life.

My Intent For Today:
1.

_____

2.

_____

3.

_____

Evening - Choose Positivity
I let the positive things in my life bring out the best in me. I strive to achieve positivity which brings me serenity.

Today I Am Grateful For:
1.

_____

2.

_____

3.

_____

October 19ᵗʰ

Morning - My Life is Mine

My problems are mine. My happiness is mine. My life is mine to live. Today I choose to live peacefully.

My Intent For Today:

1.
_____
2.
_____
3.
_____

Evening - Meditating and My Mind

Meditation allows me to quiet my mind. It allows me to focus using the peace within me to become a better me on the outside.

Today I Am Grateful For:

1.
_____
2.
_____
3.
_____

October 20th

Morning - Change My Actions

I cannot change someone else's actions. I can only change my actions. When I change my thinking, I change my words and my actions.

My Intent For Today:

1.

_____

2.

_____

3.

_____

Evening - Be Quiet

Be still and be **QUIET**

Quiet
Understanding
Is
Essential
Time

for me to keep the focus on me.

Today I Am Grateful For:

1.

_____

2.

_____

3.

_____

October 21st

Morning - The Moment of the Day
At any moment of this day, I can choose to
Feel blessed
Feel grateful
Feel happiness
Feel peaceful
Feel better
Feel free to be ME

I am the only one who has the ability to know what it is like to be me.

My Intent For Today:
1.

_____
2.

_____
3.

_____

Evening - Poise, Pause and Peace
I use my POISE to take a PAUSE and bring myself PEACE.

Today I Am Grateful For:
1.

_____
2.

_____
3.

_____

October 22nd

Morning - Having Time for ...
Today I have no time for disappointment. Today, I lower my expectations. Today I have time for serenity. Serenity means I work at staying calm.

My Intent For Today:
1.

2.

3.

Evening - Never Change Myself
I will do my best to never change myself to make others like me. If someone does not accept me for the way I am, then this person does not deserve me in the first place.

Today I Am Grateful For:
1.

2.

3.

October 23rd

Morning - I Choose Peace
Today I choose **PEACE**.
Positive
Energy
And
Compassion
Everywhere

I need **PEACE** to be my first choice.

My Intent For Today:
1.

_____

2.

_____

3.

_____

Evening - Remembering Loved Ones
Remembering beautiful memories of a loved one gone and speaking their name often keeps their spirit alive in my heart.

Today I Am Grateful For:
1.

_____

2.

_____

3.

_____

October 24ᵗʰ

Morning - My To Do List

My to do list for today:
1) Awaken with gratitude
2) Count my blessings
3) Be kind
4) Stay calm
5) Listen well
6) Love purely
7) Let go and let God
8) Sleep peacefully

My Intent For Today:

1.

_____

2.

_____

3.

_____

Evening - Patience, Faith and Hope

Patience keeps me calm. Faith keeps me strong. Patience and faith bring me hope.

Today I Am Grateful For:

1.

_____

2.

_____

3.

_____

October 25ᵗʰ

Morning - Love and Patience
Hate and anger dissipate with love and patience. The best way to dilute my anger is to show others love and patience.

My Intent For Today:
1.

2.

3.

Evening - It is All in My Attitude
My attitude influences my actions. My positive attitude leads me to positive actions. My negative attitude leads me to dangerous actions. I will watch my attitude and my actions.

Today I Am Grateful For:
1.

2.

3.

October 26ᵗʰ

Morning - My Choices

I am able to make my own choices. I choose them on my own. I move forward.

My Intent For Today:

1.

_____

2.

_____

3.

_____

Evening - Serenity, Courage and Wisdom

Acceptance leads me on the path to *serenity*. Changing gives me *courage*. Understanding brings me *wisdom*.

Three simple words I say when I need peace ... serenity, courage, wisdom.

Today I Am Grateful For:

1.

_____

2.

_____

3.

_____

October 27th

Morning - Spiritual Freedom

Every day is an independence day for me when I consider my spiritual freedom. Despite whatever human constraints are put upon my actions, I am free to think my own thoughts, creating and visualizing new ideas. I remain open to divine guidance, trusting and following my intuition.

Events from my past may linger, creating emotional barriers that prevent me from fully letting go and moving on. It is up to me to bless my past as a learning experience. It is my choice to let go, so I do. I am ready. I am willing. I am able to make courageous and mindful choices, moving forward with peace of mind and positive intentions. I thank God everyday for the spiritual freedom with which I have been blessed.

My Intent For Today:
1.

2.

3.

Evening - Giving Service

The rent for a space on Earth is paid through service to others.

Today I Am Grateful For:
1.

2.

3.

October 28ᵗʰ

Morning - I Will Make Time For ...

Today I will make time for reflection, for appreciation, for solitude, and for gratitude. Today I do not have time for worry, for anger, for argument, or for confrontation.

My Intent For Today:

1.

_____

2.

_____

3.

_____

Evening - The Gift of God's Love

When I share God's love for me with others, I am sharing a beautiful gift. This is a gift that keeps on giving. It is a gift that benefits me first and then others in my life. This is a gift that is welcomed when it is returned.

Today I Am Grateful For:

1.

_____

2.

_____

3.

_____

October 29th

Morning - Football 🏈 Terms are Tools in Life

The game of football 🏈 has many terms that are tools in life as well. For example, defense, tackle, offsides, safety, field goal, touchdown and half time. It is a team sport. There are coaches. There are rules. There are different playing positions. As much as I can have a strategy or plan, things can change and the next play can change as well.

My Intent For Today:

1.

_____

2.

_____

3.

_____

Evening - When Making Important Decisions

When I make important decisions, I do my best to keep the focus on me. I invite God to help me. I bring love, kindness and faith in. I use clear, logical and rational thinking.

Today I Am Grateful For:

1.

_____

2.

_____

3.

_____

October 30th

Morning - A Big Deal

Sometimes people say "What's the big deal?" about something I am either thinking or doing. If I do not agree with them, I no longer second guess myself. My feelings, thoughts and actions are mine and they are allowed to be a big deal to me.

My Intent For Today:

1.

2.

3.

Evening - Daily Reflection

Tonight as I end my day, I decide to accept how this day has unfolded. I choose to grow from the experiences that were not so good. I reflect from the lessons. I rejoice from the blessings of this beautiful day.

Today I Am Grateful For:

1.

2.

3.

October 31ˢᵗ

Morning - Lessons and Blessings

Happy 🦉 Halloween!

I can be haunted by the things from my past.

I can learn lessons from my past which may be helpful tools to use in my present.

Today I will not let my past haunt me.

I will use the lessons.

I will count my blessings.

I will focus on the treats.

My Intent For Today:

1.

_____

2.

_____

3.

_____

Evening - The Gift 🎁 of Life

I realize more and more that my life is a beautiful gift 🎁 that I get to share with many others. Sharing is caring and I am blessed to have others in my life who share their gift of life with me. Life is love and love is life.

Today I Am Grateful For:

1.

_____

2.

_____

3.

_____

NOVEMBER

HOPE

November 1st

Morning - Making Myself Grow

Today I will do one thing that is challenging even if it is something small. When I push myself, I make myself grow.

My Intent For Today:

1.

_____

2.

_____

3.

_____

Evening - Taking Comfort in God

In the difficult and challenging times I live through, I take comfort in knowing that God is always with me.

Today I Am Grateful For:

1.

_____

2.

_____

3.

_____

November 2nd

Morning - Smart
Today I will be smart. **SMART** means ...
Serene
Mindful
Aware
Resilient
Truthful

My Intent For Today:
1.

_____

2.

_____

3.

_____

Evening - God Loves Me
God always has a plan, a reason, a way of letting me know that God loves me. Remembering God is a way of returning all that love. Thanking God daily is a beautiful tribute.

Today I Am Grateful For:
1.

_____

2.

_____

3.

_____

November 3rd

Morning - Love, Peace, Trust and God

LOVE, JOY, KIND, CARE, PEACE, CALM, TRUST, and FAITH are all one-syllable words that HELP me become closer to GOD and GROW spiritually.

My Intent For Today:

1.

_____

2.

_____

3.

_____

Evening - Seek God

Too often I spend all of my time seeking God for answers to my problems when all I probably need to do is seek God.

Today I Am Grateful For:

1.

_____

2.

_____

3.

_____

November 4th

Morning - Disconnect from Technology

When I disconnect from my smartphone, tablet, desktop and laptop, I connect to my own technology—myself. Today I will disconnect for a period of time from technology and connect with my inner self.

My Intent For Today:

1.

2.

3.

Evening - Giving My Problems to God

Tonight, I give my problems and troubles to God. I will allow God to give me the best solutions.

Today I Am Grateful For:

1.

2.

3.

November 5th

Morning - Before Judging Others

Before I judge others, it is important to remember that some scars are not visible. Not all wounds are healed. Not all illnesses can be seen. Not all pain is obvious. I will try to remember this before speaking unkindly to someone. The outside does not always reflect the inside of a person.

My Intent For Today:

1.

_____

2.

_____

3.

_____

Evening - Faith and Hope

Having both faith and hope is the keystone to peace, serenity and tranquility.

Today I Am Grateful For:

1.

_____

2.

_____

3.

_____

November 6th

Morning - Make a Difference

The best way I can really make a difference is by being different. Today I will begin to be different and move in a better direction.

My Intent For Today:

1.

_____

2.

_____

3.

_____

Evening - Sharing My Story

When I share my experiences with someone who is open to listening, I am letting my story help them learn something that may change their lives. When I listen to another person's story, I am open to learning, too.

Today I Am Grateful For:

1.

_____

2.

_____

3.

_____

November 7th

Morning - Taking a Pause

There are so many times when I lose something like car keys or a wallet. I can immediately go into a state of PANIC. Usually if I change my thinking by taking a pause, I become calmer and am able to retrace my steps to find the thing I am missing. The same thinking can be applied to the more difficult situations in my life. So the next time I panic, I will take some deep breaths, pause, become CALM and search for what it is I am looking for. It may just be inner peace that can jumpstart the rest of my day.

My Intent For Today:

1.

2.

3.

Evening - Complete

Tonight, as the evening falls, I will be happy and proud of the things I have completed and done. I will not focus on things left undone.

Today I Am Grateful For:

1.

2.

3.

November 8ᵗʰ

Morning - Becoming Emotionally Intelligent

As I grow in becoming more in tune with my emotions, I can feel when my emotions come on. The negative emotions become clearer to me, and as I feel them rise within me, I can consciously choose to stop. Much like when I make a wrong turn while driving, make a U-Turn or take a detour, I can get my "positive thinking" on track, and head back in the proper direction. The more I practice moving away from negativity, the more emotionally intelligent I become. My emotional stamina strengthens as I continue to practice feeling my feelings.

My Intent For Today:
1.

2.

3.

Evening - Spring Forward not Fall Backward

My goal is to spring forward not fall backward, both literally and figuratively.

Today I Am Grateful For:
1.

2.

3.

November 9ᵗʰ

Morning - Owning My Emotions

In the same way I need to take responsibility for my actions, not the outcomes, I need to take ownership for my emotions. I am responsible for my happiness, joy, sadness or sorrow. No one else can take credit for my emotions except me. The power of how I feel is up to me.

My Intent For Today:

1.

_____

2.

_____

3.

_____

Evening - HELP

Tonight I will work on not hesitating to ask for **HELP**.
HELP to me means ...

Hope	**H**is
Emits	**E**ver
Laughing	**L**asting
Peace	**P**atience

Today I Am Grateful For:

1.

_____

2.

_____

3.

_____

November 10ᵗʰ

Morning - Healthy Communication

The healthiest way of communication happens when I open my ears to listen, open my mind to a new perspective, and speak from my heart with love and compassion.

My Intent For Today:

1.

_____

2.

_____

3.

_____

Evening - Different Day, Different Me

I am not the same person I was yesterday, nor I am the person I will be tomorrow. Using this logic, my relationships are not the same today as they were yesterday, nor the same as they will be tomorrow. For my relationships to be more fruitful, I work each and every day on becoming a better version of me. Some days I do better than others. The goal is to try each and every day.

Today I Am Grateful For:

1.

_____

2.

_____

3.

_____

November 11th

Morning - STOP
I love to **STOP**
Stop and be still
Take some deep breaths
Observe my feelings and thoughts
Pause and move forward with faith and hope

My Intent For Today:

1.
_____

2.
_____

3.
_____

Evening - An Attitude of Gratitude

The ability to say thank you during times of chaos, stress, pain or sorrow takes strength. Thank You, God, for what I am going through. Thank You, God, even though I may not like my situation. These expressions of gratitude create an inner peace and positive energy. Continued practice of gratitude leads me to serenity. My struggles become true blessings with time. The habit of gratitude leads to a more positive attitude.

Today I Am Grateful For:

1.
_____

2.
_____

3.
_____

November 12th

Morning - Going with My Gut

Sometimes when I make a decision, I may start to second guess my decision. Decisions made when my mind is clear, my heart is calm, and my spirit is strong, are usually good ones. Going with my gut is always good, because **GUT** to me means ...

God
Understands
This

My Intent For Today:

1.

_____

2.

_____

3.

_____

Evening - Being Kind and Gentle with Myself

Tonight, as I wrap up my day, I remember to be kind and gentle with myself. I am thankful for completing this day of my life. I acknowledge there are parts of today I will learn from and other parts that were a blessing. There were things that happened today that will be better left in today and not brought into tomorrow. There were things done right that benefited me and I will build upon those. Tonight, extending both kindness and gentleness to myself is essential.

Today I Am Grateful For:

1.

_____

2.

_____

3.

_____

November 13th

Morning - Love, Learn and Grow

I am responsible for my own feelings. By accepting this I am learning to love, learn and grow for myself. When I learn to step back, I am actually moving forward.

My Intent For Today:

1.

_____

2.

_____

3.

_____

Evening - Detach with Love

When someone's behavior or attitude is not in line with mine at that moment, the best thing I can do is to detach with love. When I detach, I am realizing that **detach** is ... **d**on't **e**ver **t**ry **a**nd **c**hange **h**im/**h**er. To detach with love is when I **love** ... **l**etting **o**thers **v**oluntarily **e**volve. This means I still love the person, but simply do not love their behavior. If I continue to engage with them, I am saying that their actions are okay with me. By detaching with love, I am able to kindly let them know how I am feeling. The detach with love concept may not always work. By trying, at least, I am able to validate how I may be feeling. It is all about the effort, not the outcome.

Today I Am Grateful For:

1.

_____

2.

_____

3.

_____

November 14ᵗʰ

Morning - Focus on the Blessings

When I focus on what I lack rather than the blessings I have, I realize how much I take for granted. In reality I actually have more blessings than I thought.

My Intent For Today:
1.

2.

3.

Evening - My Mood, My Words

A bad mood is never an excuse to use cruel words. Never. Moods pass but cruel words wound the soul. Words and tone of expression have the power to both destroy and heal. When words and tone are both true and kind, they can change my outlook on life.

Today I Am Grateful For:
1.

2.

3.

November 15th

Morning - I Appreciate ...

Today I live with the intention of expressing my generosity, kindness, and appreciation to others. I am grateful for the presence of my loved ones. I cherish the good moments and the difficulties that help me grow. As I appreciate others in my life's journey, I also feel better about myself.

My Intent For Today:

1.

2.

3.

Evening - Peace

As the days get shorter, I remind myself that I can still make the most of the day. Daylight hours may be less, but I can use my own inner light to guide me and brighten my path to happiness and peace ⏀.

Today I Am Grateful For:

1.

2.

3.

November 16ᵗʰ

Morning - God and Grace

Grace is an expression of God's love for me. Grace helps me to be grounded and brings me calmness and serenity.

GRACE is simply:

God	**G**uidance
Reaching	**R**ejuvenation
All	**A**cceptance
Children	**C**ompassion
Everywhere	**E**nergy

My Intent For Today:

1.

_____

2.

_____

3.

_____

Evening - All About Respect

Respecting others' feelings strengthens my relationships. Respecting my own feelings brings me inner peace.

Today I Am Grateful For:

1.

_____

2.

_____

3.

_____

November 17th

Morning - Judging Others

Sometimes when I judge others, it may be because they have something I want for myself. The same theory applies when I am judged. Today I will do my best not to pass judgment. Today, if others judge me, I will share my compassion and kindness with them.

My Intent For Today:

1.

_____

2.

_____

3.

_____

Evening - It is OK!

The best way to maintain my positive energy, is to do what I feel is best for me. If I do not answer a call, it is okay. If I cannot go to an appointment, it is okay. If I change my mind, it is okay. If I want to be alone, it is okay. If I take a nap, it is okay. If I do absolutely nothing, it is okay. If I decide to let go, it is okay. When I am okay, God is OK.

Today I Am Grateful For:

1.

_____

2.

_____

3.

_____

November 18th

Morning - My Happiness

Today I let my happiness be in my hands. I use my feet to walk in peace. I use my mind to keep the focus on my serenity. I use my heart to share my love. Basically, when my mind, my body, my heart and soul are all healthy, I am smiling. Being healthy and happy is my choice.

My Intent For Today:

1.

_____

2.

_____

3.

_____

Evening - What Forgiveness Brings

Forgiveness does not mean that I am accepting what was done to me was alright. It simply means that I am ready to move forward and let go of the past. Moving forward may or may not change them. Moving forward does change me.

I am tired sometimes when I am strong. I am strong sometimes when I am tired. Both situations are okay.

Today I Am Grateful For:

1.

_____

2.

_____

3.

_____

November 19th

Morning - I Am Responsible

I am truly only responsible for me. I am responsible for my thoughts, my words, my actions, my feelings, my health, my life, my gratitude, my blessings, my faith, my courage, my strength, my serenity, my peace, and my spirituality.

My Intent For Today:
1.

2.

3.

Evening - This Too Shall Pass

This too shall pass. The best way for this to happen is if I let it. If time passes, it does not mean I let the situation pass. I need to let things go and not hold onto them. This is the best way for me to truly follow "This too shall pass."

Today I Am Grateful For:
1.

2.

3.

November 20th

Morning - Being Strong

Strength comes in variations. I can be physically, emotionally and spiritually strong. I can do my best to be brave on any given day. When I do not feel so brave, perhaps I actually am STRONG for simply not feeling strong. It takes courage for a person to say, "I do not feel strong." Today I will be whatever level of strong that I can be.

My Intent For Today:

1.

_____

2.

_____

3.

_____

Evening - Experiencing Negativity

Negative emotions have a negative impact on my overall well-being. Positive emotions help me maintain my serenity and have a positive impact on my well-being. I will do my best to stay positive. If I do experience negativity, I will try to not stay with it for too long. I may even opt to not allow the negativity to enter too deeply.

Today I Am Grateful For:

1.

_____

2.

_____

3.

_____

November 21st

Morning - Listening to My Heart and Mind

I try to listen to my heart. I try to listen to my mind. If there is a conflict between the two, I pray and ask for guidance from God. This concept of looking inwards and then looking upwards helps me make good choices.

My Intent For Today:

1.

_____

2.

_____

3.

_____

Evening - How can I Help?

When someone is dealing with an issue/situation, I often ask myself the following: What is my role, if any? Will this matter a few days from now? How urgent is it? If I am to help, am I being asked for my help? If I am asked for advice, do I want to give it? Can I really give sound advice? Am I directly involved in the situation? Usually asking myself these questions helps me decide what the next right step is or can be.

Today I Am Grateful For:

1.

_____

2.

_____

3.

_____

November 22nd

Morning - When Change Comes

Whenever I try to force change to happen, it inevitably does not. When changes come slowly, smoothly, and with an inner strength, it usually works well. Change takes practice and dedication, and when it feels good, it really works.

My Intent For Today:
1.

2.

3.

Evening - What Makes Me Strong

A strong person can be one who feels their emotions. This is a person who allows themselves the time and space to work through their emotions in whatever way they feel is best for them. If they are not sure what is best, they can turn to God for guidance. Today I will do my best to be strong. If I do not feel strong and I accept this, my acceptance makes me STRONG.

Today I will strive for *strength* with my **ESPS** ...

Emotional
Spiritual
Physical
Strength

Today I Am Grateful For:
1.

2.

3.

November 23ʳᵈ

Morning - As My Day Unfolds ...

Today as my day unfolds, I will value the experiences. I will try not to force anything. I will own my actions and feelings. I will do my best to enjoy this day. I will show my compassion when necessary. I will practice kindness as often as I can. I will express gratitude often.

My Intent For Today:

1.

_____

2.

_____

3.

_____

Evening - The True Meaning of Work

Tonight, I realize the true meaning of **WORK** ...

We
Only
Require
Kindness

I now know why I love **WORK**.

Today I Am Grateful For:

1.

_____

2.

_____

3.

_____

*November 24*th

Morning - The **ABC**'s of Serenity:

Acceptance	Joy	Silence
Blessings	Kindness	Trust
Courage	Love	Understanding
Detaching with love	Maturity	Valiant
Encouragement	Nurturing	Wisdom
Faithfulness	Openness	Xtraordinary
Gratitude	Peaceful	Youthfulness
Happiness	Quiet	Zealous
Independence	Resilience	

My Intent For Today:

1.

_____

2.

_____

3.

_____

Evening - Blessings versus Problems

At the end of this day, I am grateful that my blessings outnumber my problems.

Today I Am Grateful For:

1.

_____

2.

_____

3.

_____

November 25th

Morning - A Serene Day

Today I will have a serene day. It is in my control to be serene, stay serene and share my serenity with all those whom I meet on my journey.

My Intent For Today:

1.

———————————————————————————

2.

———————————————————————————

3.

———————————————————————————

Evening - Living a Full Life

It is good to live fully. A full life may consist of: me loving someone even when they are not being/doing what I want them to; forgiving often because it helps me move forward; sharing joy and serenity with others, even strangers; lastly, bringing a smile to someone's face by simply smiling a peaceful smile.

Today I Am Grateful For:

1.

———————————————————————————

2.

———————————————————————————

3.

———————————————————————————

November 26ᵗʰ

Morning - All Kinds of Tears

When a child is born, there are tears of joy, smiles, laughter and love. When someone passes, there are tears of sorrow, sadness, frowns, and also love. It is also the same between birth and death: there are tears of joy, sorrow, smiles, laughter, sadness, frowns and love. These tears are God's way of letting me know God is present in my life always.

My Intent For Today:
1.

_____

2.

_____

3.

_____

Evening - Owning My Choices

When I make choices that truly are good for me, I do not take responsibility for the reaction of others to the choices I have made. I am owning my choices. I am accepting the outcome of my choices. I acknowledge that my choices always lead me to other choices.

Today I Am Grateful For:
1.

_____

2.

_____

3.

_____

November 27th

Morning - The Gratitude Tool

Gratitude is an amazing tool I use to keep my thoughts in a positive momentum. I am grateful for many things in my life. I am grateful for the events and people in my life that have brought me joy and happiness. Although this may sound odd, I am also grateful for the events and people in my life who have brought me pain and sadness. The reason for this gratitude is there are lessons learned from the events and people who have contributed to my pain and sadness. I learn and grow from these experiences. Thus, my gratitude. If I feel I cannot show gratitude for the moments in my life where I have suffered, then I have to turn to grace instead. Today I will express my gratitude via **HUGS**: **H**elping, **U**nderstanding, **G**enerosity, **S**erenity.

My Intent For Today:

1.

2.

3.

Evening - Focus

The good thing about looking to the past ... I can focus on and revisit the happy times and learn from the not so happy ones.

Today I Am Grateful For:

1.

2.

3.

November 28th

Morning - I Smile When ...

I smile when I am happy. I smile when I am proud. I smile when I am peaceful, I smile when I am loved. I smile because I have survived many life struggles. I smile because I can. I smile and the world smiles back at me.

My Intent For Today:

1.

_____

2.

_____

3.

_____

Evening - Because I Have Experienced

Because I have experienced weakness, I understand strength. Because I have experienced fear, I know what being brave feels like. Because I have been foolish, I have wisdom. Because I have felt pain, I can truly feel pleasure. Because I can simply feel, I can truly heal.

Today I Am Grateful For:

1.

_____

2.

_____

3.

_____

November 29th

Morning - Priceless Gifts

Some of the best gifts I can give or receive are kindness, love, attention, honesty, loyalty, peace, wisdom and serenity. These gifts are absolutely priceless.

My Intent For Today:

1.

_____

2.

_____

3.

_____

Evening - Intolerance

Tolerance for frustration is beautiful. Tolerance for disrespect is harmful. The more chances I give someone, the less respect they will have for me. They will begin to know the boundaries I set are not being fully enforced and they will know another chance will always be given. Disrespect is something I can no longer tolerate.

Today I Am Grateful For:

1.

_____

2.

_____

3.

_____

November 30th

Morning - Peace ☮

Peace ☮ is more a verb than a noun. Peace is not a thing, it is an action. Peace is not a place of quiet, solitude or calm. Peace is being who I am in the midst of noise, chaos, strike, trouble or hard work with crazy deadlines, and still have calm and serenity in my heart and mind.

My Intent For Today:

1.

2.

3.

Evening - I've Had To …

I've had to fail to find success. I've had to make mistakes to learn. I've had to be hurt to be brave. I've had to experience love to understand heartbreak. I've had to have pain in order to forgive.

Today I Am Grateful For:

1.

2.

3.

DECEMBER

SPIRITUAL
BREAKTHROUGH

December 1st

Morning - Ten Questions Lead Me to a Deeper Me
These ten questions lead me to deeper thoughts.
1) Who am I?
2) What do I want?
3) What is my purpose?
4) What brings me joy?
5) What brings me peace?
6) What brings me happiness?
7) What am I grateful for?
8) What does God want from me?
9) What is God's plan for me?
10) Am I willing to accept God's plan?

My Intent For Today:
1.

_____

2.

_____

3.

_____

Evening - Giving Gifts
It is the season of giving gifts 🎁 to those whom I love and care for. It is therefore even more important to give myself a gift ... the gift of love and care for self. When I practice giving myself the gift of love and care, I can share this gift with others.

Today I Am Grateful For:
1.

_____

2.

_____

3.

_____

December 2ⁿᵈ

Morning - Let it Snow!

When I watch the first snowfall, I am overcome with the feeling of **HOPE**. The snow falling, pure and white, pretty, and the flakes, each one so beautiful, is like a blanket of white light protection covering me. Watching the snow brings out the happy child in me. I find peace in catching snowflakes on my tongue,

making a snow angel on a fresh bed of snow,

taking a walk and enjoying the beauty,

sitting in a sunny spot outside and feeling the warmth of the sun on my face,

drinking a cup of hot chocolate outside,

or talking selfies of my joy being in the snow.

Today I will enjoy the beauty of the snowfall and open my mind, body, heart and soul to the spiritual teachings of the winter season.

My Intent For Today:

1.

_____

2.

_____

3.

_____

Evening - Who I Am

I am learning more and more each day not only who I am, but also whose I am. I am a child of God always.

Today I Am Grateful For:

1.

_____

2.

_____

3.

_____

December 3rd

Morning - Winter ❄

In the dead of winter ❄, the snow turns to ice in freezing temperatures. Similarly, I can become frozen in certain situations if I notice when the temperature begins to rise, the ice slowly melts. Similarly, I am human and can slowly become "unfrozen" by taking deep breaths, finding my calm and serenity, and asking for guidance from God or others whom I trust.

My Intent For Today:

1.

_____

2.

_____

3.

_____

Evening - Lose My Fear, Find My Faith

When I keep God in my mind, I have no time for fear. When I am afraid, I am leaving God out of my thoughts. In other words, I lose my fear by finding my faith.

Today I Am Grateful For:

1.

_____

2.

_____

3.

_____

December 4th

Morning - Be Open to Activity

Today, I will be open to activity and activating my mind and body. Motion can dictate emotion. When I am fearful, depressed or discouraged, I may stay still, or stay in bed, or remain inactive. When I am happy, confident, or overjoyed, I may be more inclined to be active physically, socially, or even spiritually.

My Intent For Today:

1.

_____

2.

_____

3.

_____

Evening - Silent Gratitude

Silent gratitude is the purest form of giving. Being a good listener leads me to silent gratitude. I am able to be present in the moment for both myself and the person to whom I am listening.

Today I Am Grateful For:

1.

_____

2.

_____

3.

_____

December 5th

Morning - Working Spiritual Overtime

When people work overtime, they reap financial benefits. When people work overtime in their relationship with God, they reap spiritual benefits. These spiritual benefits certainly come in handy **"OVER TIME."**

My Intent For Today:

1.

_____

2.

_____

3.

_____

Evening - Perfection versus Serenity

When I struggle for perfection, my serenity can be jeopardized.

Today I Am Grateful For:

1.

_____

2.

_____

3.

_____

December 6ᵗʰ

Morning - It Begins with Me

If I want certain things to be, I have to realize, it begins with ME.

My Intent For Today:

1.

_____

2.

_____

3.

_____

Evening - Who I Am And Who I Want To Be

I am the only one (except for God) who knows who I am and who I want to be going forward. The four things that contribute to this are: my thoughts, my words, my actions, and my spiritual connection to God.

Today I Am Grateful For:

1.

_____

2.

_____

3.

_____

December 7ᵗʰ

Morning - Accepting My Flaws

When I accept my flaws, I am trying to improve myself. My flaws become a part of my past. The improved me is part of my present.

My Intent For Today:

1.

_____

2.

_____

3.

_____

Evening - Sanity, Serenity and Happiness

For me, sanity can be saying to someone who I disagree with, "You may be right!" This choice of action helps me maintain my own serenity and happiness.

Today I Am Grateful For:

1.

_____

2.

_____

3.

_____

December 8th

Morning - Today I Will

Today I will communicate with love and kindness. Today I will complain less and pray more. Today I will let go of any negative thoughts. Today I will seek God as my source of strength. Today I will open my heart to this beautiful day of love and life. Today I will rejoice and be grateful. Today I will share my hope and faith with others.

My Intent For Today:

1.

_____

2.

_____

3.

_____

Evening - Learn to Love Myself

The most important thing I can do to improve any relationship is to learn how to love myself rather than abandon myself.

Today I Am Grateful For:

1.

_____

2.

_____

3.

_____

December 9th

Morning - My Breath Guides Me

Sometimes all I need to do is to close my eyes and just breathe. I let my breath guide me away from where my mind takes me.

My Intent For Today:

1.

_____

2.

_____

3.

_____

Evening - My Body and Mind

Tonight I will learn to be present in my body rather than be stuck in my mind and avoiding my feelings. My body will direct my mind, not vice versa.

Today I Am Grateful For:

1.

_____

2.

_____

3.

_____

December 10ᵗʰ

Morning - Sending Positive Thoughts and Peace

Today, as I begin my day, I send positive thoughts, energy, love and well wishes to those in my life whom I care about. I also send peace out to my community, country and the world, as we all can use peace.

My Intent For Today:

1.

_____

2.

_____

3.

_____

Evening - Ask for Peace

Tonight, as my day comes to a close, I can sleep more peacefully knowing I am praying and sending positive energy to those whom I care about. I have gratitude for the day that is over. I ask for peace for those in the world who do not have peace. I pray for those who have no one to pray for them.

Today I Am Grateful For:

1.

_____

2.

_____

3.

_____

December 11th

Morning - Inner Strength

Sometimes I define my inner strength as how I handle life's uncomfortable situations. Inner strength can be something as simple as giving up a seat on a train for an elder person, even when I want to sit; drinking a glass of stillwater when I want a carbonated beverage; smiling at people I really do not like despite my inner resistance; going for a walk when I much rather watch TV while lying in bed. Inner strength can come from something that is so simple.

My Intent For Today:

1.

_____

2.

_____

3.

_____

Evening - Motivation and Energy

When my motivation is lagging and my energy is sagging, I turn to You, God. Your presence motivates and relaxes me as I try to sleep.

Today I Am Grateful For:

1.

_____

2.

_____

3.

_____

December 12ᵗʰ

Morning - Love, Compassion and Kindness

Today I will shower love, compassion and kindness on myself first and then on everyone I meet. I will be grateful for any love, compassion and kindness I receive today.

My Intent For Today:

1.

2.

3.

Evening - Thank the Universe

I thank the universe for the good things in my life and for the goodness my life brings me.

Today I Am Grateful For:

1.

2.

3.

December 13ᵗʰ

Morning - It is Good to ...

It is good to be a giving person, but not to the point of being used. It is good to show love, but not to the point of my heart being abused. It is good to trust, but I will not be naïve. It is good to listen, but it is important to not lose my own voice.

My Intent For Today:

1.

_____

2.

_____

3.

_____

Evening - Preparing for Tomorrow

When I get myself ready for bed and a peaceful night's sleep, I also prepare myself for a wonderful new day that comes with tomorrow. I thank God as I fall asleep for tonight and tomorrow.

Today I Am Grateful For:

1.

_____

2.

_____

3.

_____

December 14th

Morning - Simply Me

Today, as a new day begins, I will feel my feelings. I will see clearly. I will speak kindly. I will act with compassion. I will love freely. I will accept. I will understand. I will simply be me.

My Intent For Today:

1.

2.

3.

Evening - The End of the Day

At the end of this day, I reflect on how I felt, how I spoke, how I acted, how I loved, how I accepted, how I understood, and how I simply was being me.

Today I Am Grateful For:

1.

2.

3.

December 15th

Morning - God's Will

God, show me what Your will is for me. Show me if the decision I am about to make is in my best interest. Show me if there is a better path for me to explore. Thank You, God, for all You will show me today.

My Intent For Today:

1.

_____

2.

_____

3.

_____

Evening - Walking Away

Walking away from people who have hurt me helps me realize my strength and self-worth. Walking away is not a sign of weakness. It is a way of me realizing how valuable and strong I really am.

Today I Am Grateful For:

1.

_____

2.

_____

3.

_____

December 16th

Morning - A Good Day

What makes a really good day for me? A good day is when I am maintaining my serenity, staying tolerant while being in frustrating situations, sharing kindness with others, and showing love to family and friends. Today will be a good day for me.

My Intent For Today:

1.

_____

2.

_____

3.

_____

Evening - Mistakes

I do not want to judge myself for the mistakes I make. I want to be proud of myself for how I move forward and correct the mistakes I make.

Today I Am Grateful For:

1.

_____

2.

_____

3.

_____

December 17th

Morning - The Little Child in Me

When I am feeling nervous or anxious, I realize it may be the little child in me coming out. When I am feeling happy and giddy, that too could be the little child in me. This little child has a place and time to make a guest appearance. I welcome the little child in me to share this day.

My Intent For Today:

1.

_____

2.

_____

3.

_____

Evening - Spirituality Is ...

Spirituality is simply about understanding who I am. It is not about what I believe. Spirituality is the knowledge of the Great "I AM." Spirituality is being present in me "NOW." Spirituality is accepting myself where I am and who I am at this moment. Spirituality is about being in true alignment and peace with God, my Creator. When I am one with God, I have absolute spirituality. Spirituality is where I release EGO and focus on GOD.

Today I Am Grateful For:

1.

_____

2.

_____

3.

_____

December 18th

Morning - Being Present

My healthiest relationships are the ones where I can be truly present and in the moment with the person I am with. This also holds true for my relationship with God. My relationship with God is healthiest when I am truly present. God is present for me all the time. Basically, the best gift I bring to this spiritual relationship is me being present.

My Intent For Today:

1.

_____

2.

_____

3.

_____

Evening - My Scars

Every battle scar tells a memory and a story. The wound may heal and the scar that remains is a symbol of the strength I have shown to come through. Some of my wounds are not visible to others, as they are wounds of the heart. These wounds also heal. They do leave invisible scars. My scars make me stronger in faith.

Today I Am Grateful For:

1.

_____

2.

_____

3.

_____

December 19ᵗʰ

Morning - Do Something Nice for Someone

The simplest ways to do something nice for someone without them knowing is to:

Pray for them

Send positive energy and thoughts out to them

Have compassion for them

Forgive them

Love them

My Intent For Today:

1.

_____

2.

_____

3.

_____

Evening - To Act, React or Under-react

Sometimes when I act impulsively it is because I am either excited or afraid. These actions are more likely reactions, not initial actions. I am learning to take a pause before I react, or to simply pause before I act. This helps me act or react with conviction and it leaves out the drama. Another option I have is the ability to under-react by simply doing or saying—NOTHING.

Today I Am Grateful For:

1.

_____

2.

_____

3.

_____

December 20ᵗʰ

Morning - Morning on Earth
It is a beautiful morning on earth and I am blessed by all those who love me and all whom I love.

My Intent For Today:
1.

_____

2.

_____

3.

_____

Evening - My Praying 🙏 Hands
My hands are often folded for prayer 🙏. I have often pondered why. One hand represents the five senses: sight, hearing, touch, taste and smell. The other hand represents the five powerful and potential enemies of the mind: lust, anger, greed, desire (undo attachment/ jealousy) and ego (arrogance). The folding of the hands displays a sense of humility and a true devotion to the Divine Spirit. I will try to keep all these ten influences in balance and submit to God with a clear mind. Praying 🙏 with folded hands keeps me in close connection with the Divine Spirit.

Today I Am Grateful For:
1.

_____

2.

_____

3.

_____

December 21ˢᵗ

Morning - Daylight and God's Light

Today is the shortest day of the year, meaning the least amount of sunlight/daylight. On this day, I especially rely on God's light to guide me and keep me warm. After this day, the daylight becomes longer, which makes me happy. I can also rely on my own inner light of peace and happiness to guide me.

My Intent For Today:

1.

_____

2.

_____

3.

_____

Evening - Tonight as I Sleep

Today was the shortest day of the year. This meant the least amount of sunlight. This is the first day of winter. To me this means each day going forward is getting longer and spring and summer are coming. If today has the least amount of sunlight, I have the most amount of night light to sleep. I place my concerns with God tonight as I sleep. I will rest peacefully as I sleep knowing God will handle my concerns better than I can. I will enjoy my sleep and look forward to a longer period of sunlight starting tomorrow.

Today I Am Grateful For:

1.

_____

2.

_____

3.

_____

December 22ⁿᵈ

Morning - My Mind, My Space, My Breath

Today I will do my best to keep any negative influencing thoughts from renting long-term space in my mind. Positive thoughts can stay in my mind rent free.

When life seems simply too much, it is best to really BREATHE. After all, the next moment of life is simply a breath away. The breath keeps us focused on us and not the "stuff" of life.

My Intent For Today:

1.

_____

2.

_____

3.

_____

Evening - Release to God

Tonight, as I lay myself down to sleep, I release my resentments, fears, frustrations, worries and negativity at God's feet. I ask God to take them and bring me a tomorrow full of newness and hope.

Today I Am Grateful For:

1.

_____

2.

_____

3.

_____

December 23rd

Morning - Choosing Kindness

When I express kindness, I am showing my strength and self-confidence. When I am rude, I am showing my insecurities and weaknesses. It takes even greater discipline to be kind to those who are rude to me. Those who have a strong sense of self are able to express kindness with ease. Today by choosing kindness over being right, I will be right every time as my kindness is a sign of strength and self-discipline.

My Intent For Today:
1.

2.

3.

Evening - My Friends

Some of the best gifts 🎁 this holiday season are MY **FRIENDS!**
My friends ...
Feed me
Respect me
Inspire me
Encourage me
Nurture me
Deserve me
Strengthen me
Thank you to all my friends.

Today I Am Grateful For:
1.

2.

3.

December 24ᵗʰ

Morning - God Give Me ...

Today, God, give me strength when I feel weak. Give me faith when I feel fear. Give me Your power when I feel powerless. Today, God, I am trusting You, just as You always trust me.

My Intent For Today:

1.

_____

2.

_____

3.

_____

Evening - Tonight's Prayer

Tonight, as I end my day, I pray. I pray for my loved ones, which includes me. I pray for the world and all those in it. I pray for a good night's sleep, knowing that my soul is God's to keep.

Today I Am Grateful For:

1.

_____

2.

_____

3.

_____

December 25th

Morning - The Many Meanings of GIFT 🎁

GIFT 🎁 means:

Give	God	Grow
It	Is	In
Forward	Faithful	Faith
Today	Today	Together

My Intent For Today:

1.

_____

2.

_____

3.

_____

Evening - Peace ☮ on Earth

Tonight as I quiet my mind, I focus on seeking more peace ☮ on earth. The simplest way to do this is to work at having inner peace. Inner peace is what is needed to be passed on to others in my home, in my community, and to my friends. The ripple effects of inner peace go out to the world of people I come in contact with.

Today I Am Grateful For:

1.

_____

2.

_____

3.

_____

December 26ᵗʰ

Morning - Bring Me Through
Today, when my motivation is lagging and my energy is sagging, I turn to God, to bring me through.

My Intent For Today:
1.
_____
2.
_____
3.
_____

Evening - Peace
Tonight as I close my eyes to sleep, I ask God to give me peace. I hope to awake refreshed and ready to begin another day of numerous blessings. I will awaken with a joyous smile and inner peace.

Today I Am Grateful For:
1.
_____
2.
_____
3.
_____

December 27th

Morning - Taking Care of Me

The time I spend on my smartphone and on social media could be better spent sharing love and kindness with others.

Random acts of kindness actually release more endorphins in me for inner peace, more strength and increased serenity.

Today I will do my best to take care of me. The best care is when I am not trying to control and when I am not being controlled. Staying balanced is the best way for me.

My Intent For Today:
1.

_____

2.

_____

3.

_____

Evening - Simple Reminder

When I do not think I have enough, or when I feel I need more to make me happy, I remind myself of others who do not have as much as I do. This simple reminder brings me humility. This also helps me to be more thankful for even the little things. I express my thanks to people for their thoughtfulness.

Today I Am Grateful For:
1.

_____

2.

_____

3.

_____

December 28th

Morning - Using My Breath

When I feel stress, I take a few moments to sit in the silence of prayer. I begin by letting go of negative thoughts and focus on the comforting idea, "Do you need me? I am here." I relax the muscles in my face and neck. I let my shoulders drop and keep my hands loosely in my lap. I let my chair support me. I relax and simply be. I breathe in Divine love and unconditional acceptance. I exhale peace, serenity, and harmony. Bringing myself back from these brief meditations, I feel refreshed, ready to return to my day with a positive and peaceful attitude.

My Intent For Today:

1.

_____

2.

_____

3.

_____

Evening - Being Late

It is disrespectful when I show up late to a function, business meeting or appointment. It appears as if my time is more valuable. It shows a lack of appreciation of others' time and sends a message that they are unimportant. For tomorrow, I will do my best to be on time.

Today I Am Grateful For:

1.

_____

2.

_____

3.

_____

December 29ᵗʰ

Morning - Being Kind and Gentle

When I blame myself, I am not being kind and gentle to myself which can actually create feelings of shame or guilt. This can lead me down a dark path. It is better to stay in the light, which means being kind and gentle to myself.

My Intent For Today:

1.
_____

2.
_____

3.
_____

Evening - My Life, My Truth

I do not let the fear about the future consume my life. I simply just live for the here and now. I have faith the right things will fall into place.

The truth is sometimes I just have to do what is best for me and my life, not what is best for everyone else.

Today I Am Grateful For:

1.
_____

2.
_____

3.
_____

December 30ᵗʰ

Morning - The Year Ahead

The year ahead has 525,600 minutes. It is up to me to decide how I want to spend those minutes. For all the minutes I focus on negative thinking or express negative emotions, I lose minutes of serenity and gratitude. I will do my best to use the 525,600 minutes wisely and maintain my serenity, gratitude and faith in the healthiest way I can. I will focus on staying healthy: physically, emotionally, mentally, spiritually, and financially.

My Intent For Today:

1.

_____

2.

_____

3.

_____

Evening - Asking God for Things

The year that is coming to a close has had 12 months, 52 weeks, 365 days, 8,760 hours, 525,600 minutes, 31,536,000 seconds of time (except for the leap years, 😂 LOL). Upon reflection, there were moments of happiness, craziness, crisis and sadness. These moments brought me to today. I am most grateful for being alive today.

In doing service for others, I often find answers to my own questions, and I find solutions to my own problems.

Today I Am Grateful For:

1.

_____

2.

_____

3.

_____

December 31ˢᵗ

Morning - Gratitude Resolution

Today is the last day of the year. Some take today to make a resolution for the New Year. The most realistic resolution for me to make is to be the best me I can be each and every day. Another simplistic resolution is to practice daily gratitude by writing one thing I am grateful for. If I do this daily, I will form a good new habit of gratitude which will lead me to more happiness and serenity.

My Intent For Today:

1.

_____

2.

_____

3.

_____

Evening - Wishing for a Peaceful New Year

When I wish everyone on the planet a happy, healthy and peaceful new year, I am sharing my love with my fellow humans. I hope the new year will be a year of positive changes and kindnesses expressed to loved ones and strangers alike. Life is an amazing gift 🎁 and God always has a plan. I do my best to continue to have faith, hope, love and patience, especially since God has so much faith, hope, love and patience with me.

Today I Am Grateful For:

1.

_____

2.

_____

3.

_____

Congratulations to ME, I have achieved 1,098 intentions and 1,098 gifts of gratitude!

Acknowledgments

Thank You God for the gift of life, breath, heartbeat, mind, body and spirit.

God is the One I need to acknowledge, first and foremost. My Creator, Planner, Guide, Protector, Partner, Eternal Parent and Spiritual Leader to bring me Home 🏠.

I honestly believe I was closest to God when I was in utero. Once I was able to breathe on my own, I needed to reconnect to God, as my spiritual journey and life's journey began.

My parents, Kamla and Mohan Makhijani, and my two other parents, Toto Bhambhani (my dad's best friend) and Lakhu Makhijani (my mum's youngest brother) gave me their wisdom, courage, acceptance, serenity, love, and presence in my life and were wonderful role models for myself and my beautiful big sister, Shannon (Sunita).

My sister, Sunita Makhijani, who genuinely wanted a little sister and has been a vitally important role model and a wonderful traveling buddy in my life. My drive, determination, and desire to compete were all influenced by the high benchmarks of excellence Sunita did not even realize she had set for me. So much so that we both sound alike, have identical handwriting, and even complete each other's sentences. We are twins 👯 ♊ born five years apart.

I acknowledge every single life experience I have had, especially during the years from 2008 through 2021. The struggles of my life that have strengthened me, instilled a deeper faith, brought me closer to God to the point of **being totally in love with God**, and have given me so much serenity. Specifically, the morning of July 26, 2020 when my trust in God skyrocketed and I witnessed a true miracle which was God's Hands at work.

There are so many other people in Shaleen's life who have touched me in ways that have been so meaningful to me.

- My childhood friends in Hollis Hills, my classmates at P.S. 188 and J.H.S. 172, my many teachers at these two institutions; my TMLA sisters during 1980-1984 and the many nuns and lay teachers there; my St. John's University family of friends; my camp friends and counselors at Shibley Day Camp during the summers of 1978—1980. The groups of people mentioned here are the ones who contributed to helping me grow as a student, friend and camp friend.

- My friends from college helped me to find my career path (namely Chris, Mary Ann, and Mike). My Indian Subcontinent Student Organization (ISSO) friends and childhood family friends made me appreciate my heritage and shared the joy of my teenage and young 20's with dance parties, adventures and hanging out.

- My maternal grandfather, our family priest, my mum and my dad all helped me develop my moral barometer, my spiritual quest, and my deeper understanding of what being a Sindhi Hindu was all about. My dad nurtured my spirituality and my mum taught me the religions traditions. They both taught me that all religions share the same God and that God's Hand is always upon my family. My sister taught me how to be passionate about wanting to enjoy life, play and travel. She also shared her love of studying with me.

- My two beautiful nieces and handsome nephew, Sheena, Kristen and Alec whom I love just like my own children. As their revered "Masi" (mother's sister, aka, their second mum), I have spoiled them, challenged them, encouraged them, taught them, supported them, and played endless hours of games with them. I have even learned from them. I am blessed and honored to be their Masi and now a "Nani Masi" to my grandnephew, baby Bryce.

Another group who needs my sincere gratitude is the wonderful women I call "The Racqueteers," sixteen strong women from my hometown of Port Washington. My Racqueteers (Racs) sisters: Mary Ann, Dottie, Lisa, Mala, Maggie, Ilene, Ruth, Geri, Lori, Jody, Eve, Suzan, Joanie, Dipika, Nina with whom I have played many hours of tennis, shared many dinners and brunches with, and laughed with at many birthday and holiday celebrations. Two of these Racs, namely Vicki (Schnicki) and Karen, whom I lost in September and October 2015 (three weeks apart), taught me many important life lessons about raising my sons, accepting life's situations, and the bravery of facing cancer head-on.

My BFF, Ronda, an amazing lady who shared her love for country music with me and has traveled to many concerts and to tennis camp. We laugh, cry and support each other.

Our closest family friends, Monica, Pankaj, Meenakshi and Shiv, as well as Seema, Arjun, Gaj, and Shubi, who have spent many weekends and vacations together creating beautiful memories, sharing laughter and fun.

I have long ago realized that I must be an old soul as many of my close friends are older and wiser than I. My church family and travel buddies, namely Elaine, Chris, Jan, and Doreen have also contributed to my spiritual growth. Andrea, Cristina, Jayne and Lee Anne have also shared part of the journey.

Elaine is the lady I owe an immense amount of thanks to. She had enough faith in me to ask me to take over a weekly silent prayer and meditation group in 2012. Fast forward to March 17, 2020—the COVID-19 pandemic struck, and I created a Zoom platform for the guided meditations that I had been leading since 2012. The meditations were offered three times daily. Many of the participants were known to me from various areas of my life and others were complete strangers. I give thanks to Linda, Lawrence, Julia, Enid, Stuart, Roy, Anne, Brenna, Carol, Mary Lou, Carole,

Marilyn, Frank, Terry, Wendi, Barbara, Teresa, Helen, Susanne, Susan, Margaret, Laurie, Sara, Sue, Julie R., Kishin, Lena, Julie K., Maureen, Louise, Richard, Nathalie, Michelle, Lucianna and countless others. My own spiritual connection deepened to a new level through the guided meditations with "The Beloveds" meditation group.

A special thank you to Syrah for transcribing my thoughts into a manuscript, to Karyn for helping me with the copy editing, and to Linda and Shaan for their assistance with finalizing the layout.

A sincere note of appreciation to Stephen Matthews, Kali Hammond and Katie McCray at Page Publishing for their dedication and assistance in producing my vision.

A final acknowledgment to all my friends and family with whom I have shared my "Shaleen thoughts ⟁" over the last ten years. Each of you, and you know who you all are, are the real supporters and influencers who encouraged and inspired me to create the vision that led me to compiling these inspirational thoughts into a book to be shared with others. Let the sharing begin and know that the best is yet to come.